Praise for *Fiv*

GW00675104

"A brilliant book. *Five Brain Leadership* ... you think about yourself and your team, while giving you the tools and strategies you need to transform your habits to become an effective leader. Clearly argued and thoroughly engaging."

CASIAN GLAVCE, vice president, Canada, C.R. Laurence Co., Inc.

"Carlos Davidovich has written an accessible, straight-talking read on how each of us can tap into and harness the power of our brain. This book is a joy to read and speaks to the potential we all have and how to celebrate it and liberate it. A must-read!"

ANNIE TOBIAS, CEO, Proximity Institute (Ontario Hospital Association)

"Carlos Davidovich brought neuromanagement to me in the form of a practical guide, but beyond that has enabled my mind (which I now understand better!) to connect the dots with thoughts about energy, time, purpose, vision, diversity, and the development of a learning culture that I need to create successful change. This is my first essential business book read of the year!"

MICHAEL CHIVERS, CHRO, Titan Cement; founder, Chivers People & Change

"I come from a background in neurological psychology and have a passion for all sciences. Yet, I am genuinely humbled by Carlos Davidovich's ability to articulate his understanding and real-world application of such a complex subject so entertainingly!"

LARRY CASH, founder, SuccessFinder personality assessment; co-author, *Personality DNA*

"Brilliant, straightforward, and with a practical set of exercises. Simply love it."

ALEKSANDRA PFENING, head of unit service implementation
(risk IT department), Deutsche Börse Group

"If you are looking for a science-backed, practical guide to explain you why you behave as you do in different situations, this book is must-read."

LUBOS LUKASIK, chief commercial officer, Enterprise, and board member, T-Mobile Czech Republic a.s.

"This is a solid resource for leaders who strive to build fluency in creating conditions for growth and thriving at work. *Five Brain Leadership* is full of undeniable evidence anchored in the field of medicine, and it includes actionable strategies that have the potential to transform interpersonal dynamics."

HAESUN MOON, PhD, executive director, Canadian Centre for Brief Coaching, University of Toronto (Canada); author, *Coaching A–Z*

"This is an excellent and informative book with a great blend of science and real-world application. Carlos Davidovich connects the dots between neuroscience and everyday life in the business realm. *Five Brain Leadership* is packed with resources and provides you with practical information about how science can help us understand our interactions and improve our performance—and transform us from good leaders to great leaders!"

LATA VISEU, director, professional development, Human Resources Professionals Association

**FIVE BRAIN
LEADERSHIP**

FIVE BRAIN

Carlos Davidovich, MD

with Jennifer Elizabeth Brunton, PhD

LEADERSHIP

HOW NEUROSCIENCE CAN HELP YOU MASTER YOUR INSTINCTS AND BUILD BETTER TEAMS

PAGE TWO

Copyright © 2023 by Carlos Davidovich, MD

All rights reserved. No part of this book may be reproduced, stored in a retrieval system or transmitted, in any form or by any means, without the prior written consent of the publisher, except in the case of brief quotations, embodied in reviews and articles.

Some names and identifying details have been changed to protect the privacy of individuals.

This book is not intended as a substitute for the medical advice of physicians. The reader should regularly consult a physician in matters relating to his/her/their health and particularly with respect to any symptoms that may require diagnosis or medical attention.

Excerpts from *You Are Not So Smart* by David McRaney are used with permission from Penguin Random House LLC.

Cataloguing in publication information is available from Library and Archives Canada.
ISBN 978-1-77458-273-2 (paperback)
ISBN 978-77458-274-9 (ebook)

Page Two
pagetwo.com

Copyedited by Melissa Edwards
Proofread by Alison Strobel
Cover and interior design by Cameron McKague
Interior illustrations by Michelle Clement
Indexed by Donald Howes

carlosdavidovich.com

To all those giants who let us step on their shoulders to see further, and to our clients, who trusted and taught us through their sharing, experiences, and outcomes.

Contents

INTRODUCTION

Why People—and Leaders—
Need Neuromanagement

H OW MUCH do you know about your brain? Do you want
to know more? I myself would like to know how to leverage its power in my daily life—to keep my mind sharp; to
grow wiser and more astute in my thoughts, words, and
actions; to become more effective, productive, and satisfied
at work. I want to learn how to apply all of the information
that is available in a practical way, to become less biased and
more comfortable with change, to thrive as a leader and help
my team do the same. If we're on the same page, let's walk
this path together.

During the pandemic, I spent my time offering webinars
on what was happening to all of us, especially in terms of
the emotional impact and how to overcome it. I worked with
clients on regaining and *retaining* their well-being despite
everything that was going on. I became even more convinced

that knowing about our neurology and how it affects our behavior can make a crucial difference in our work and in our personal lives. With the right approach, we can avoid so many of the hazards that contemporary life causes in our brains, while actually increasing our neural strengths and agility.

Over the past few years, neuroscience has moved from the remote province of scientific laboratories into the beating heart of educated conversation. We are now able to leverage extensive knowledge in the field to fine-tune and augment our interpersonal and professional lives like never before. And we can be sure that many more groundbreaking and potentially revolutionary neuroscientific discoveries are on the horizon.

Someday soon, we may even be able to answer some of humankind's most profound questions, many of which are directly tied to that most cherished organ: the brain. We all have a basic curiosity about who we are, about the meaning of life, and about the ultimate destination of the human race. If you're reading this book, you probably share my deep interest in the wonders of the human brain. It, however, remains in many ways a puzzle, mysterious to say the least.

So far, we can only study the human brain in very limited ways. We do so, in general, by introducing variables and then observing the ensuing results. Such approaches frame the brain as a "black box"—an impenetrable object from which only input (stimulus) and output (response) can be discerned.

In other words, we cannot yet examine the processes in the brain itself that happen in between variable and result. What exactly does the path from A to B look like? How do the mechanisms involved actually work? How many more details would we be able to discern if we could develop the ability to truly access the intricate workings of the brain?

In short, despite the breadth of our anatomical, biological, and chemical knowledge, we have not yet penetrated the

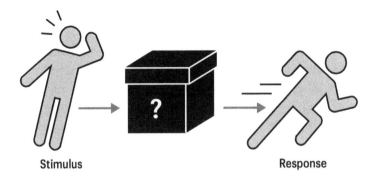

Stimulus   **Response**

brain-based processes that define us as human beings. What we are currently able to do is, quite simply, not enough. Yes, we can say that we know a lot about the brain when compared to what we knew in the past. And, every day, our knowledge grows by leaps and bounds. But the biggest questions are still before us. Unless we are able to make a quantum leap to a bold new way of thinking about how our brain works—and how to study it—there is still a long way to go.

But what if we could find a shortcut for understanding the key functions of the brain? The Human Brain Project—a ten-year effort initiated in 2013 at universities, teaching hospitals, and research centers across Europe—is just one of many scientific endeavors underway across the globe that is trying to decipher these mysteries and unlock the secrets of what we call "consciousness." Through the work of these dedicated teams, brain research has begun to grow exponentially. Current and future findings from this burgeoning field hold enormous potential for humanity as we begin to breach this compelling and challenging frontier.

My purpose here is not to write about that ongoing science, per se. The aim of this book is to connect the dots between neuroscience and daily life in the business sphere:

and the heart of that intersection is neuromanagement. Think of this as a handbook for your brain at work.

I'm going to provide you with practical, operationalizable information about how science can help us understand our interactions and improve our performance. More specifically, we will explore together how to apply the latest insights from neuroscience and related cognitive behavior techniques to turn good leadership into great leadership.

That is the essence of neuromanagement: the fusion of relevant discoveries in neuroscience with best practices in leadership and management. We will see how leaders who are able to integrate brain science into their management methods gain an invaluable edge—and build stronger, more dynamic relationships, enterprise-wide and beyond.

In this exploration I will try to bridge both worlds: to connect the realm of scientific research with the sphere of our daily work. The sciences are constantly churning out information that could benefit organizations in many ways. But that useful knowledge is often couched in complicated, inaccessible terms. In order to create a meaningful conduit, I'm going to offer a fresh, practical take on the vast amount of completed and in-progress work being produced by outstanding scholars and researchers in neuroscience. I'll provide a range of pragmatic perspectives and proactive tools gleaned from cutting-edge research and designed to spark growth. I'm convinced that, by understanding how to apply this new information to your organization and your business, you will yield invaluable opportunities.

How exactly can we use neuroscience to change our lives for the better—and make our work as leaders more rewarding and productive? I'll explore that question at length throughout this book, with an eye toward sharing crucial information about how the brain, body, and mind work together in real-life situations.

You see, the more we know about how we function, the better we can deal with ourselves and with those for whom we are responsible. We can learn how our neurology impacts every aspect of our lives, from individual behavior and health to job performance and satisfaction. We can deploy neuromanagement insights to improve communication, productivity, resilience, and more. Moreover, we can learn to maximize our potential in every aspect of our lives by taking full advantage of this remarkable machinery that we call the human body. There is so much to be learned from its almost perfect way of functioning, all of which is dependent on our complex, fascinating, magnificent, multilayered brain.

The Decade Of...

For the past three decades, the international bodies that name the most significant events or advancements of a given decade have chosen themes that are either directly or closely related to neuroscience. The revolutionary discoveries and public dialogues about the brain that took place in the 1990s led the U.S. Congress and the National Institute of Mental Health to name that era "the Decade of the Brain." The 2000s were named "the Decade of Behavior," thanks to progress in the social and behavioral sciences, and the 2010s became "the Decade of the Mind" to honor an ongoing international project of the same name that, as explained by neuroscientist James Olds of the Krasnow Institute for Advanced Study at George Mason University, "seeks to harness science across multiple disciplines to discover how human 'mind' emerges from the biological activity of human brains."

Brain, behavior, mind: each picks up where the others leave off. When we think of brain functions, we think of perception, motor control, thoughts, and action. We don't typically

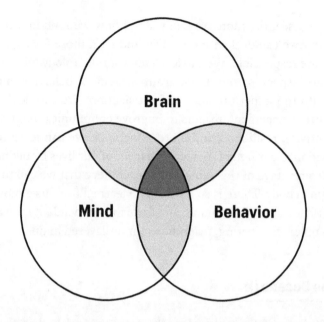

include seemingly mind-related human experiences, such as love, kindness, or gratitude. But these less-quantifiable phenomena are all domains where neuroscience is not only making progress, it is actually breaking through traditional boundaries between the sciences and the humanities. And human behavior—the focus of the decade between Brain and Mind—emerges as yet another expression of the extensive brain-body-mind connections that scientists, philosophers, and other curious people continue to explore today.

With all of the energy behind these closely intertwined subjects, it's no surprise that there's a wealth of scientific information just waiting to be mined for practical, effective wisdom and tools. So, it's time to build bridges. In the pages to come we're going to connect the dots—between the sciences, between science and business, between ourselves and our brains, between leaders, colleagues, and employees.

My Path to Neuromanagement

Medicine was my doorway to the working world. But—as is true in many professions—those of us in the medical field often find out that what we study in medical school can be very different from what we end up doing in our post-school life. Once I finished my training in internal medicine, I began a fast-paced existence that often felt like a race. My course ran through the paths of medicine, business, and psychology, as well as an intense process of—and investment in—self-development.

Finally, after many, many years, I found two related activities that offered me peak enjoyment: giving lectures and workshops on neuromanagement, and practicing executive coaching. With these, I have been able to bring together my diverse personal and professional interests: medicine, business, psychology, and human inner development.

Throughout this process, what has fascinated me most has been to observe how pathways that we once conceived of as entirely unrelated are intersecting in ways that show they're very much connected. This integration of different sources of knowledge gives us unique opportunities to get closer to a coherent, holistic understanding of the big puzzles of our lives.

In this realm of emergent connections, my wealth of experience allows me to bring a unique perspective to the evolving field of neuromanagement. We can use leading-edge neuroscience research into human behavior in executive coaching and leadership in organizations because these fields interpenetrate each other in myriad, constantly evolving ways. This is the basic starting point of what I hope to convey in the chapters that follow.

For years I have conducted workshops, lectures, and webinars all over the world, mainly to people working in

companies. All of my presentations involve linking daily situations at work with how the brain functions. My goal is to
raise awareness and understanding of human behavior—why
we react in certain ways, why relationships can be so complicated, and, in the end, what leads our work in a positive
or negative direction. Over time, I've realized that the way
I *connect* the knowledge I have with the workaday world is
new—and it changes people's lives.

At the end of every workshop or talk I give, the most
common question I hear is about where to find the information I've just presented. The truth is, though, that all along
I've been bringing together this information from many different sources.

In other words, it's simply not possible to find the information that I present in my workshops in any one book
currently in publication. Eventually, I realized that I needed
to bring all this knowledge together myself. There is no need
for others to walk the same complicated path that I've trav-
eled in order to arrive at the same place. From here, I hope,
those who are inspired by what they read in these pages will
take these tools and use their own knowledge and experience
to boost neuromanagement to the next level.

Organizations and the Brain

Through my own two decades of experience with leading
people and leading *myself*—along with my work in listening
to other leaders and observing radically different leadership
styles across many countries and regions—I've been able to
learn about the many barriers and difficulties in the leadership world that transcend specific cultures or business sectors.

One of the most frequent types of statements I hear—and
I've heard this all across the globe—regards the perception

that the problems afflicting a given organization are unique. "This happens only in our company," I'm told. Or, "Carlos, to be able to exactly understand the difficulties in our company, you need to be working here for a while."

These two sentences have been repeated like a mantra at just about every company where I've offered my services as a coach or consultant.

Of course, in the moment, I usually ask for details. And in each specific case, what the issues always amount to is essentially the same problems and difficulties, the same story, as I've encountered at every other organization, worldwide. The challenges organizations and businesses confront are not about areas, companies, countries, or languages; they're not even about any unique enterprise. They're always about people connecting—or not connecting—with other people. We all share similar experiences, everywhere. For the most part, however, we don't know it.

There is no doubt that we believe, and on some level need to believe, that we are different, special; that what happens in our company only happens in our particular company. It's very hard to convince people that actual differences across human relationships and behavior are quite minimal. But it's true.

As we learn more and more about how our brain functions, one thing has caught my attention: It seems to me that we tend to unconsciously project our brain's inner organizational system on outside organizations. Nevertheless, as actors in the workplace, we are still far from the perfection of our biological processes. As we gain a deeper understanding of the wonders of the brain, so too will our knowledge and expertise around brain-work connections deepen. A thoughtful examination of the parallels between these realms is yet another compelling, potentially fruitful facet of neuromanagement I will explore.

Our brain still has so much to teach us. Are we going to be intelligent enough to understand its intricate processes? Are we going to be able to decipher its secrets? Perhaps we need to be open-minded enough to accept new ways of "reading" those processes. The more we know, the more we will probably need to challenge our prior hypotheses and habitual assumptions on an ongoing basis.

This holds especially true for the workplace, where most of us spend the majority of our waking hours. By incorporating innovative neuromanagement practices and understanding our whole brain in all five of its manifestations, extraordinary leaders can make a real difference for their work environment, the individuals who inhabit it—including the C-suite—and even the bottom line. In a time when the next pandemic or global crisis could be just around the corner, these brain-smart individuals and workplaces will, in turn, have the skills and, even more importantly, the resiliency to tackle challenges and to welcome transformation.

Through the chapters that follow, you will journey from learning how to understand and manage your own brain via neuromanagement to learning how to apply these techniques to drive positive change in your organization. Along the way, I'll introduce you to key scientific concepts and show clearly how those concepts relate to your daily work environment. And I'll explore the many ways leaders can deploy neuroscience-derived insights in their management skill sets. To further facilitate constructive transformation, each chapter includes a handy tool (or more than one) designed to help you spin your knowledge into action.

Let's dive in together!

How Many Brains Does It Take to Run an Organization?

THE FINER POINTS of what, exactly, constitutes a brain, not to mention how many brains we actually have, might seem like something only scientists—or, more precisely, neuroscientists—are qualified to discuss. These days, however, it's important for everyone to have a basic conception of our brain (and by that I mean our multiple brains) in order to better grasp the biological tools available to us. In this chapter, you'll learn about how our multiple brains work together, and you'll come to understand their properties, potential, and applications in our daily lives.

Increasing our awareness about ourselves helps us evolve as human beings. For the purposes of this book, it will also lead us to the next level in understanding how we interact with each other, and the reasons behind our reactions and behaviors in the working world.

Let's go back to the original question: How many brains do we have? As with so many other complex matters, the answer is: It depends.

One or More Brains?

The number of brains we may be said to possess depends on how we define the brain. If we are thinking about the organ that is located inside our skull, we could certainly say that we have a single brain. That would be one correct answer.

Or, if we follow Roger W. Sperry's late 1970s description of the brain, we could say that we have two brains. Sperry, who was awarded the 1981 Nobel Prize in Physiology or Medicine for his work on the split brain, was the first person to identify and define the different and specific functions of each brain hemisphere. The two brains Sperry described in actuality consist of one brain with two highly specialized sides: the left, or rational brain; and the right, or creative, emotional brain.

This general concept will be familiar to many, but the scientist also went further by attributing some key functions to each hemisphere. According to Sperry, the left brain is home base for rational and linear thinking. This hemisphere is mainly in charge of storing precise, concrete information. For example, it is where our knowledge of the alphabet is located, but not our grasp and use of language. Thanks to the pioneering work of Jack Gallant—the neuroscientist who created a map of language in the brain and whose name now graces the Gallant Lab at the University of California, Berkeley—we now know that the latter is widely distributed throughout.

The left brain is also the area from which our understanding of abstract numbers emerges. It's mostly thanks to the left brain that we are able to organize all of the information we take in and retain. It's the place where what we call "the comfort zone" resides, too. In other words, the left brain is responsible for—and inclined toward—behaviors and responses that are known and habitual, and, thus, "comfortable."

By contrast, in Sperry's model, the right side of our brain can move us beyond our comfort zones because it is the main seat of imagination and creativity. It's also where holistic thinking takes place: this hemisphere helps us understand patterns and see the big picture. In part, this is because the right brain constantly works as a sort of radar. It's always checking what is happening around us, ready to detect any threatening situation and preparing us to protect ourselves.

This side of the brain does not perceive time, at least in the way we understand it. It is in a permanent state of being in the present moment, which is why memories from the past and fears about the future have such a strong impact on us. When our emotions are triggered, it feels as if everything is happening right now. In our right, or emotional, brain, that which we call the past, the present, and the future all happen at the same time.

Nowadays, all of Sperry's concepts are under evaluation. Some aspects of his findings remain correct, but we also have new information. We now believe that we need both hemispheres for most of the functions he described, from imagination to rational abilities. Furthermore, the sides of the brain actually have to be very well connected for each such process to occur. Yet there still does seem to be a clear distribution of tasks: the left hemisphere sees the tree, while the right hemisphere sees the forest.

How about Three Brains?

Then again, we might argue that we have three brains, in line with physician and neuroscientist Paul D. MacLean's triune conception of the brain. MacLean found that the natural process of evolution did not replace earlier brains with later, more evolved versions. Instead, it added one over the other, starting from the first manifestations of life all the way up to our current form.

The Triune Brain Hypothesis

| **Reptilian Complex:** | **Paleo-mammalian Complex:** | **Neo-mammalian Complex:** |
| Instincts, aggression, and basic bodily needs/desires | Emotions, motivation, and belonging behaviors | Language, planning, and abstract thought planning |

What I'm getting at is that inside our skull we still possess the most primitive manifestation of a biological brain. A relatively simple brain that snakes, lizards, and crocodiles retain, which, of course, is called the reptilian or lizard brain. This reptilian brain is located right at the base of our skull. It performs very basic functions and essentially operates on black and white principles, with no recourse to shades of gray. This brain maintains an archaic behavioral program, the same as that possessed by snakes and lizards.

In humans, this brain oversees our balance, muscles, and other autonomic functions, such as breathing and maintaining a heartbeat. It's the system responsible for self-defense when we feel threatened—otherwise known as the "fight-flight-freeze response." It also regulates eating, sleep, and sexual behavior. In brief, this brain is related to sustenance, survival, and sex.

This brain is rigid, structured. It is filled with ancestral memories and genetically shaped responses to stimuli that stem from the beginning of life as we understand it. In fact, this brain has existed for 500 million years. Thanks to its protective mechanisms, we were able to survive as a species. So, we trust this brain—or, at least, it's the one we trust the most. And it still plays a very important and active role in our daily behavior.

The second brain, following MacLean's triune model, is the one we inherited from large mammals, such as horses and apes. It's officially called the limbic system or paleo-mammalian brain, but it's often known by its more popular moniker: the emotional brain. This brain is concerned mainly with the more evolved feelings we call emotions.

I've already described the right hemisphere as the part of the brain that's in charge of our emotions, and the right brain is indeed the executor or initiator of those emotions, the place where feelings are designated in response to thoughts or circumstances. But the limbic system, or emotional brain, serves as the headquarters of our emotions. In essence, it's the primary place from which our emotions—which are in fact very broadly distributed throughout our bodies—are administered.

Stimulation of this part of the brain by a mild electrical current produces the basic emotions (joy, fear, rage, pleasure, pain, and so on). It appears to be the primary seat of attention, affective memories, and emotions. While our emotions are distributed throughout our whole body, the limbic brain is the command center for management of these emotions. This second brain has been around for about 200 million years—not as many years as the reptilian brain, but quite a long time, nonetheless.

The third and last brain in the evolutionary process, following MacLean's model, is one that developed primarily and most fully in humans. Technically, this brain is called the prefrontal cortex, or the superior or rational (neo-mammalian) brain. This brain is where our higher cognitive functions reside.

MacLean referred to it as "the mother of invention and father of abstract thought." Relatively speaking, the prefrontal cortex is a high energy consumer, devouring massive quantities of the necessary fuel (glucose) to carry out all those specialized functions.

This ravenous, remarkable, uniquely human brain has been with us, much as we know it today, for 100,000 years. Obviously, that's a much shorter span of time compared with how long the earlier two have been around. And we know that our survival as a species is due not to the more recently evolved rational brain, but to the reptilian brain. So, in a very basic, natural way, the reptilian brain remains the one that we trust and rely on most. In any situation in which we feel fear or sense danger, our reptilian brain will take over. It's very difficult to stop this instinctive reaction when we are facing challenging or dangerous situations, unless we are very well trained (think paramedics or firefighters).

Even More Brains!

Do you know where the most powerful magnetic and electrical fields in the body reside?

When I ask this question in my workshops, most people guess they're in the brain. When I tell them that's incorrect, their second response—without any hesitation—is the heart.

In 1991, professor of physiology J. Andrew Armour announced that he'd detected the presence of thousands of neurons in the heart. He referred to them as "the little brain in the heart." His findings don't necessarily mean that the heart has consciousness (thinking, imagining, reasoning), only that it has neurons. The mind, as we currently understand it, is still limited to the brain that resides inside our skull.

But it's still an amazing discovery. The neurons in our heart not only receive orders and information from the upper brain, they send back a lot of information, too. This is a new area of investigation, and a lot of research will be needed to understand the purpose and functioning of these heart neurons, which make up a fourth "brain" in the human body.

One promising area of study involves the connections between heart health and mental health. There are several heart-related medical situations that seem to be linked to psychological conditions, but we don't yet have enough information to draw solid conclusions. For instance, there is a high incidence of depression and symptoms related to other psychological issues in patients who have experienced almost any kind of heart problem, be it cardiovascular surgery, issues with the circulatory system, a cardiac transplant, or a cardiac arrest. Statistics show that up to 15 percent of patients with cardiovascular disease and up to 20 percent of patients who have undergone coronary artery bypass graft surgery experience major depression.

Another interesting and related case of looking beyond the heart's blood-pumping function has as its protagonist Richard Davidson, a professor of psychology and psychiatry at the University of Wisconsin–Madison. Davidson was the main researcher in a project designed to study the effects of long-term meditation on the brain.

In his book, Davidson describes how the Dalai Lama introduced him to his main study subjects, a group of Buddhist monks. Davidson first explained to the monks that his study was intended to analyze the effects of long-term meditation practice. He then told them that he was going to study their brains, in order to observe the potential changes caused by meditation. At that moment, the monks started giggling. Davidson asked them why they were amused, and they explained that they thought he was looking at the wrong organ. If he wanted to discover the effects of long-term meditation, they said, he should study their hearts.

Many cultures and languages also frame the heart as more than just a pump. For instance, in English, we express that we remember something really well by saying, "I know it by heart," right? Did you ever consider what that phrase is literally expressing? Basically, we're saying, "I know something so well that it is *in my heart*." Very curious, to say the least. Similarly, in Spanish, the word for "to remember" is *recordar*. Its etymology comes from the Latin root *recordari*, which combines *re* (again) with *cordari* (heart). In order to remember, we need to go through our heart to retrieve any information. This can be found in French as well: *par coeur* ("by heart").

The ancient Greeks and Romans believed that what we call the mind was located in our heart. These days, we contend that the mind is housed elsewhere (again, usually in the brain). But perhaps there is a bit of truth to the ideas of those long-ago philosophers? Or maybe they knew something that we've forgotten over time?

A Fifth and (for Now) Final Brain

The fifth and last brain is the one located in our digestive system, our gut. There are more neurons—100 million, to be precise—in our intestines than in our whole spinal cord. As with the heart brain, we cannot consider the gut brain as a mind, per se. But its influence on the upper brain is nonetheless very clear.

"Spilling my guts," "gut feelings," "butterflies in my stomach": I'm convinced there's something to these traditional expressions. Aren't you? The neurons in our digestive system are definitely feeding us information via what's often called the "gut-brain axis." But of what sort?

"The [gut] brain doesn't help with the great thought processes... religion, philosophy, and poetry are left to the brain in the head," said Michael Gershon, an expert in gastroenterology, author of *The Second Brain*, and chair of the Department of Anatomy and Cell Biology at NewYork-Presbyterian/Columbia University Irving Medical Center. But despite an apparent lack of "great thoughts," the intricate functions of our digestive system are no less important for our survival and well-being. And those functions must be maintained—by the dedicated neurons dispersed throughout, which constantly monitor gut health and activity. "Thus equipped with its own reflexes and senses, the [gut] brain can control its behavior independently of the brain," Gershon has explained.

The intimate connection between our moods and our digestive system is well known. A bidirectional influential process links the two: any change in our mood may affect the way our digestive system is working, and any process that affects our gut can alter our mood.

Another unexpected and revelatory finding regarding this fifth brain? Researchers discovered that 90 percent of our serotonin, a neurotransmitter involved in the process of happiness, is produced in our digestive system. Maybe in the near future psychiatrists will take care of our guts as well!

Even now, any medication used to treat depression must work not only through the big brain in our skull, but also through the gut brain. The reason for this is that every medication used to treat depression has a similar objective: keeping a good level of serotonin in circulation, as long as possible. Given that the gut is the main producer of serotonin, the role our fifth brain plays in mental health is crystal clear.

Our Brains, Business, and the Real Boss

Have you noticed that, out of all five of those brains, only one—the prefrontal cortex—relates to what we call rational thinking? The other four are primarily interacting with, or fueled by, our emotions and instincts. In other words, 80 percent of the input we are receiving is linked with our emotions or with the way we perceive our emotions.

It's funny: so often in the business world, I hear people say, "We are very rational." Of course, we aren't! And there's even more evidence of our less-rational inclinations: all five of our brains are involved in our decision-making processes, but the final weight of our decisions—consciously or not—lies in our emotions.

This notable discovery was put forth by Antonio Damasio, a respected neuroscientist and professor of psychology, philosophy, and neurology at the University of Southern California. In his book *Descartes' Error: Emotion, Reason, and the Human Brain*, he describes the process by which his research led him to such a surprising conclusion. What he found, in short, is that our rational and emotional brains have to be connected if each is to function properly. And when it comes down to it, he found, our emotions—not reason or rational thought—are the boss of this complicated, interconnected system!

Sharing Damasio's groundbreaking findings is one of the most enjoyable parts of my presentations. Saying that our emotions have the final word in our decisions is, no doubt, a very provocative statement. So, once I mention this idea to an audience, I remain silent for a moment. I like to give people time to process—and to observe how they digest this novel information.

Years ago, when I first started to deliver this news, I was very cautious. Frankly, I was kind of afraid of how people might react; I was waiting for pushback. Well, that never happened! I don't mean that everyone always completely accepts the whole concept, but at least they're willing to consider it. I suspect that my medical background gives me credibility in this arena, since, at the very least, my audience doesn't question the validity of the professionally vetted concept itself. Eventually, in one way or another, people typically see some truth to Damasio's contentions.

Still, in our current business world, it's very difficult to accept the fact that emotions play a key role when we make what we see as highly rational decisions. After all, we need to believe that we ourselves are primarily rational beings, or, in other words, that we are in control.

I've presented this concept many times to audiences composed of people with backgrounds in finance. I initially expected this population to be the most difficult to convince of the crucial roles our emotions play in our decisions. Over time, though, I've found that this hasn't been the case.

Nonetheless, I am occasionally asked to substantiate my point. In such cases, I always give the same example: If I present you, my entire audience, with a spreadsheet showing the financial state of a given company, would you all agree on how those figures should be understood? Would you all interpret that spreadsheet in the same way? The response when I pose this question is a unanimous "No!" Any interpretation, even of mathematical figures, is touched by our emotions, and shaped by a subjective understanding of the data that's based on our past experiences and many other factors.

One roadblock to processing this information is that the word "emotion" has very negative connotations in the business world. When we say that someone is "emotional," we mean it in a negative way—generally in reference to a person who is not able to manage or control their emotions. But what

I'm talking about here is a perspective that frames emotions as more universal and ubiquitous than most people in the business world take them to be.

Temple Grandin and Catherine Johnson make a similar distinction in their book, *Animals in Translation*:

> We humans tend to think of emotions as dangerous forces that need to be strictly controlled by reason and logic. But that's not how the brain works. In the brain, logic and reason are never separate from emotion. Even nonsense syllables have an emotional charge, either positive or negative. Nothing is neutral.

The emotions we all invariably experience can work in very subtle ways. Because of this, we are not always consciously aware of all the emotions we are feeling. Emotions also exist on several planes, from internal feelings and external expressions of those feelings to the pervasive and ever-present ways they influence our behavior.

With four out of five brains solidly on the emotion "team," it's no wonder that we have our work cut out for us if we want to proactively harness those energies to make better decisions and enhance our work relationships and environments. Helping leaders take these factors into account is an overarching goal of my work. After all, in the words of Donald Calne, the Canadian neurologist who first used dopamine to treat Parkinson's disease, "The essential difference between emotion and reason is that emotion leads to action while reason leads to conclusions."

Again, this is not a new concept—however eye-opening it may be in the contemporary business sphere. The words "emotion" and "motivation" actually have the same Latin root, *movere* ("to take action"). Companies that understand this concept orient their marketing messages toward impacting emotions, rather than toward rationally explaining the characteristics of their products. Still, there's a long way to go before most enterprises truly understand and integrate the emotional angle in their business practices. To that end, I teach an entire neuromarketing course in the MBA program at the University of New York in Prague on this concept alone.

A major financial consulting company called Grant Thornton has even embraced this emotion-forward approach in their marketing messages, placing the power of emotion (in the form of "instinct") front and center in its ads. Take this example I've spotted in various places across Europe:

> Business decisions are rarely black and white. Dynamic organizations know they need to apply both reason and instinct to decision-making... This is how we advise our clients every day.

Effective, right? Yet it is so rare to see companies in this sector leverage such emotional components in their marketing campaigns.

The automotive industry, on the other hand, is deeply invested in connecting emotions with its products. Automobile companies understand that promoting cars by touting engine features or other technical characteristics won't inspire or persuade consumers. Every top brand produces marketing materials that reflect the impact of its cars on human emotions. I highly recommend watching automotive ad campaigns on YouTube—you'll see what I mean. In my workshops, I present a fantastic video from Audi, in which the marketing message is: "What is technology for, if not to awaken emotions?"

Because our emotions are fundamentally central to who we are and *who we want to be*, ads that sell positive, desired feelings sell cars. Gaining an awareness of how our five brains work in such contexts and beyond can help us grow in every capacity—as marketers, but also as leaders, consumers, individuals. When we start to become cognizant of how profoundly our emotions shape our seemingly rational thoughts and behaviors, interesting patterns start to emerge.

Here's a striking example: we know that the fundamental organizing principle of the brain is to minimize danger (things that make us feel threatened or unsafe) and maximize reward (things that make us feel happy, satisfied, safe, and so on). We also know that the fundamental organizing principle of most companies is to minimize risk and maximize results. In essence, we've taken the same principle that steers our brains and projected it outside of ourselves to shape the central tenets of our organizations. As we begin to truly comprehend the amazing five brain complex that can produce such results, we can learn to harness its tremendous powers to extraordinary effect.

Five Brain Leadership

Deploying insight into our ordinary yet astounding multiple brains is increasingly the key to training innovative, effective leaders. Those in leadership roles must learn to skillfully integrate the activities of this network of brains to meet—and exceed—performance expectations. We need our rational brains to set strategies. But we also need our emotional brains to engage effectively with others. And we sometimes need our gut brains to take risks when faced with challenges—even when the rational brain is not yet on board.

In our current age of rapid change, strong, agile leadership skills have never been more valuable. Many words come to mind when we think of an ideal leader: rational, logical, decisive, single-minded. But do these stereotypical leadership qualities really reflect the capacities that the leaders of today—and tomorrow—need to cultivate? As we've seen, the latest findings from neuroscience would suggest otherwise. In truth, great leaders think not just with their brains, but with their heart and gut, too.

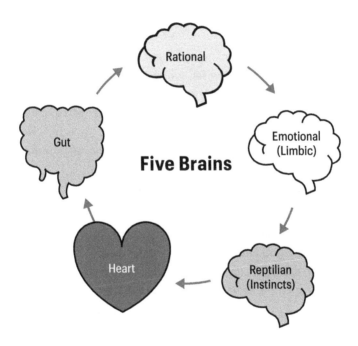

Moving forward, let's keep in mind Antonio Damasio's idea that humans are not rational beings that feel, they are emotional beings that think. We are emotional beings with brand-new rational software that we still don't really trust. Armed with unprecedented knowledge and tools, however, we can teach ourselves to evolve further in myriad ways.

PRACTICES TO NURTURE AND CONNECT YOUR FIVE BRAINS

Here are some strategies I recommend for leaders who want to build their complementary capacities in all five brains. Each exercise takes only a few minutes, can be practiced in a variety of settings, and helps to hone and integrate your various brains.

EXERCISE 1: Heart and Gut Brain Feelings

Build confidence in listening to your gut and heart—two educated advisors that only grow wiser over a career of experiences and challenges. What we call gut or heart feelings might seem magical. But our digestive and heart brains, like our upper brain, actually work based on very complex algorithms. These algorithms work with tons of data loaded into the system—and the system encompasses our entire life.

STEP 1: Start small. Bring to mind a minor decision that's on your plate.

STEP 2: Now, think of one possible course of action. Try to take stock of how you feel when you mentally "decide" to follow this route. On a concrete level, pay attention to your breathing, heart rate, and stomach, as well as to any detectable emotions that arise.

STEP 3: Now consider an alternate choice. How do your feelings change?

STEP 4: Can you discern which decision your heart and gut brains lean toward? These feelings may be very subtle, but in time and with practice you will begin to recognize and honor your instinctual, physiological-emotional responses.

EXERCISE 2: Translation

Leaders who are higher in the organization often allow gut feelings to play a more important role in making final decisions. But those at every level need to train themselves to listen, understand, and trust their non-rational sources of information.

Practice taking time to "translate" the activities of your emotional brains into the language of your rational brain. Through repetition, you'll master a quick, easy way to maximize the potential of your five brains by translating your emotional reactions into reasoned ideas and actions.

STEP 1: First, you'll need to accept this concept in order to develop the capacity for translation. There is simply no doubt that you are constantly receiving information from different parts of yourself. You don't need to know exactly where it's coming from, just accept that it's available—and then listen to it.

STEP 2: Think about a current work challenge. What information or ideas come up first? These won't necessarily be "right," but they will be a product of the two algorithms that react first. That is, you'll initially receive a mixture of information from your gut and reptilian brains. Next, write down whatever information/ideas you perceive at this stage, even if you're not clear on how they are related or might be implemented. Sit with your ideas a bit longer to sense if your heart brain or emotional brain have anything to add. Write down these impressions as well. As you practice this exercise, you'll be developing your understanding of the languages of your multiple brains. You will start seeing where your thoughts come from, what the triggers are. This can be very useful information!

STEP 3: Now, invite your rational brain to weigh in. Using logic and objectivity, balance the pros and cons of your most reasoned response. Arrive at the best rational decision.

STEP 4: Craft a final decision. The optimal course of action will most likely incorporate a combination of your rational and non-rational approaches.

2

From Overwhelmed to Flourishing: Put Your Oxygen Mask On First!

TRESS, STRESS, STRESS: it seems this word has come to represent the paradigmatic condition of our time. Whoever we are, whatever our job, wherever we live, stress is at the center of many conversations in our daily lives. We use it as a shield to explain why we don't feel like our best selves at work and at home. For all of our many brilliant brains, we just can't seem to escape this pervasive aspect of contemporary life. Stress is like a dark cloud hanging over us, ready to hit us at any time—unless we're already buried under it.

Now that we've learned about the brain, let's look at the brain on stress. In this chapter, I'll introduce you to the fundamental terms and concepts behind my Thriving Formula—a set of tension-busting techniques that we will delve into in Chapter 3. These tools will enable you to give your brain what it needs for you to lead yourself, and *then* the people on your team and in your organization, from a state of stressful brain fog to the pinnacle of thriving neurological health.

Our bodies are amazingly complicated and naturally intelligent instruments. If we want to do better with the challenges of daily life and to function at our best, we need to learn about and then take advantage of our physiological cycles and responses. Here and in the following chapter, you'll gain indispensable insights and tools for optimizing both your personal well-being and your professional performance by making the shift from overwhelmed to flourishing.

If you're reading this book, you're probably a high achiever, someone who's driven to excel. Over the years, you've likely developed patterns and strategies that you think help you succeed—and I'll bet you believe that stress is a natural, inevitable outcome of your high-pressure, highly productive life. Guess what? We can do better than that. We can draw on the latest findings in neuroscience and other fields (and, occasionally, some ancient wisdom as well) to evolve away from these patterns—and still succeed beyond our wildest dreams.

This chapter will lay an extensive foundation for the insights and tools you'll find in the rest of the book, starting with information that will help you transform a perpetual state of feeling overwhelmed into a healthy way of being, or flourishing. It builds on valuable scientific findings about human physiology, with fresh ways of looking at how we spend our time and energy—and it will offer practical exercises to take your performance to the next level, just by making a few key changes. Chances are, you will see yourself reflected in many of the stress-inducing habits described; luckily, you'll also gain a plethora of actionable health- and productivity-enhancing tips that you can easily integrate into your schedule.

The truth is, most of us don't understand the real meaning of stress. We mix it up with so many other physical and emotional phenomena that don't belong in the same bucket at all. In fact, experiencing stress is normal! Hard to believe, right? What's more, without our physiological stress response, we would die. Stress is a normal physical mechanism that's designed to protect us. It also helps get us moving when movement is called for.

What we normally refer to as stress is actually the excess of this basic bodily response, which should technically be referred to as *distress*. The importance of this stress-distress distinction cannot be overstated. In *The Upside of Stress*, author Kelly McGonigal describes a *Health Psychology* study that tracked 30,000 adults in the United States over eight years. In 1998, as part of that year's National Health Interview Survey, participants were asked the following questions: "How much stress did you experience in the last year?" and "Do you believe that stress is harmful for your health?"

Over the following years, the researchers correlated the survey findings with National Death Index mortality data. People who had claimed to experience a lot of stress in the health survey had a 43 percent increase in their risk of dying. But—and this is the interesting part—this increase only applied to those who also believed that stress was harmful for their health. Individuals who experienced a lot of stress but didn't think stress was harmful were not more likely to die. What's more, they had a lower risk of dying than anyone else in the study, including people who had relatively little stress.

Extrapolating from these results to the larger U.S. population at the time, the researchers estimated that, during this eight-year period, an average of 20,000 people died a premature death each year in association with the belief that stress was bad for them. That is, something about this way of thinking was linked with an increased risk of premature death, whether through a helpless attitude, impact on the immune system, or other related phenomena. The researchers concluded, however, that, with increased understanding, it's possible to change the way your body responds to stress.

One way to avoid the negative consequences of fearing that stress is bad for you is to educate yourself. Most of the physical manifestations of stress represent healthy bodily responses that are intended to help us deal with difficult situations in life. For instance, an increase in your heart rate or speed of breathing represents a body mechanism that distributes more oxygen and blood to the parts of your body that need those resources to face strenuous external circumstances. In other words, such physical changes are preparing us to perform better. These body reactions are highly evolved, healthy preparations for confronting negative situations in our environment, be it the wilderness of our forebears or the boardrooms and executive suites of today.

In my workshops, and in this book, I prefer to replace this commonly overused and misconstrued term with the word "overwhelmed." This term involves not only stress, per se, but also the many other physical and emotional manifestations of the ways we respond to challenging circumstances or events. These various components of the overwhelmed state typically prevent us from accessing our inner equilibrium. My personal experience in teaching this subject has taught me a great deal about how people perceive the concept, so I want to share some key insights from my workshops with you.

I always try to start my presentations by finding out what people think or believe in regards to the topic I'm about to present. This knowledge gives me a lot of useful information that helps me refine how my presentation might best unfold. When I'm covering this chapter's topic, I begin by asking the workshop audience a few questions related to the feeling of being overwhelmed. First, I start with this question: "What does being overwhelmed mean to you?" What follows are the most frequent responses I hear.

Lack Of...
- Control
- Perspective
- Knowledge
- Familiarity
- Understanding
- Stability
- Sense of being in the comfort zone

Too Many/Too Much...
- Tasks
- Expectations
- Competing demands
- Negative chaos
- Running in all directions

Inability To...
- Focus
- Prioritize
- Make decisions
- Cope emotionally

Once the workshop participants have expressed their feelings and experiences, I present a simple and clear definition of feeling overwhelmed: *Feeling completely overcome by emotions.*

Next, I ask them to describe specific situations in which they have felt overwhelmed by their profession or their clients. The most frequent responses are:

- The collapse of a deal
- Quarter-end pressure and constant interruptions

- Competing priorities
- High volume of emails requiring a response
- Report cards
- Having to fire someone
- Balancing home and working life
- Too many client calls + anger + immediate deadlines
- Deadlines + children + a new operating system
- Team at capacity + large-scale downsizing

There are tons of other examples; our working lives are filled with situations that are difficult to handle. This is mainly because, much or even most of the time, we are essentially being hijacked by a torrent of simultaneous emotions that blurs our understanding and overshadows our sense of being in control. This constant bombardment of energy triggers a domino effect on our capacity to function (and feel) well in some or all of our various roles at work and beyond. If you're reading this book, you probably know just what I am talking about.

After this, I ask my participants to describe the state of being overwhelmed in detail. How do they feel physically and emotionally when they are overwhelmed? These are the responses I hear:

Emotional
- Anxiety
- Fear
- Lack of concentration and focus
- Feeling frozen
- Mental fog
- Messiness
- Oversensitivity
- Grouchiness
- Confusion

- Persistent anger
- Short-temperedness
- Abnormal crying
- Inability to distinguish thoughts from reality
- Helplessness
- Overreacting to situations that are objectively not as stressful as they appear

Physical
- Tingling
- Eating disorders
- Sleep disturbances
- Pounding/racing heart
- Sweating
- Headache
- Joint pain
- Bowel dysfunction
- High blood pressure
- Blurred vision
- Shortness of breath
- Increased perception of wrinkles
- Increased sensitivity to infections and illness
- Stomachache

The answers given to this question fascinate me because, as might be expected, people's descriptions of their emotional and physical manifestations of this state closely mirror those found in the medical literature.

And the list goes on and on! Asking this question of the group allows participants to hear each other's responses and to realize that they are all in the same boat. I'm guessing their replies may resonate with you as well.

Next, I ask, "What actions do you take to overcome this state?" To that question, the responses I usually hear include:

Holistic

- Visualizing positive outcomes
- Practicing gratitude
- Revisiting a frustrating story from a more positive perspective
- Practicing various mindfulness techniques
- Spending time with a pet
- Meditating
- Praying
- Reading
- Doing something altruistic

Work-Related

- Prioritizing certain activities
- Writing a "to-do list"
- Delegating
- Negotiating
- Putting things in perspective by asking, "What's the worst that can happen?"
- Asking, "What can I learn from this experience?"
- Connecting at the watercooler
- Turning phone off
- Reframing the situation

Health

- Healthy eating
- Physical exercise
- Taking a break
- Breathing techniques
- Bouncing a ball
- Listening to music
- Resetting expectations
- Walking

Other

- Talking it out
- Drinking
- Spending time with children/family
- Retail therapy
- Having sex
- Laughing

As different as they may seem, every single one of these responses is oriented toward the same objective: buying time. This is not by chance. Remember the triune brain theory from the previous chapter—MacLean's finding that, from an evolutionary perspective, we have three brains: the oldest, or reptilian, brain; the limbic, or emotional, brain; and the rational brain, or prefrontal cortex. Every bit of information that comes to us from the outside world always reaches all three brains. But there is one slight yet crucial difference in how it does so: timing. First, that information will impact the reptilian brain. A fraction of a second later, the emotional brain will receive the very same information. Finally, another fraction of a second later, the prefrontal cortex, or rational brain, gets in on the news.

The question is, why? The answer is actually quite simple: survival. Out of all of our brains, the reptilian brain is the best prepared for reacting to danger, enabling us to defend and protect ourselves in the shortest time possible. When something dangerous threatens us, we urgently need that survival reaction—our fight-flight-freeze response—to be in charge. If, instead, the rational brain was the first to be aware of the situation, we would be in deep trouble. At such moments, we don't need to think. We need to act—quickly!

This time lapse between parts of the brain can have both positive and negative effects. Let's say, for example, we receive a misleading or aggressive email. If our reptilian brain gains control of us in the moment, things can become overly complicated. We might make the mistake of responding to that email right away, without thinking. We might even respond in "reptilian" language. Driven by our most primal brain, we've escalated the situation—neither a healthy nor productive way of dealing with things. Similar scenarios can arise in so many contexts: during a tough conversation, when the mistakes of others affect our work, when we're not able to meet deadlines, when we receive reports that don't meet our standards or requirements, and so on. And on and on.

That's why each and every one of the techniques we employ to overcome an overwhelmed state is about buying time, thereby allowing the necessary information to reach our rational brain. Only then are we prepared to make a rational decision. Once we've created that temporal space, we are able to choose to respond in a more proactive, positive manner—whether to that unfriendly email or to any other challenging situation.

My last question is this: "What does flourishing mean for you?" Most typically, my participants describe this as feeling:

- In control again
- In a state of flow
- In a groove
- Capable again
- A sense of accomplishment
- Energized
- Peaceful
- Happy
- Balanced
- Present

- Motivated
- In "the zone"
- In tune
- A mind-body connection
- On top of things
- A can-do attitude
- Engaged

As you can see, there is no need to have a profound or scientific knowledge of the process of being overwhelmed to understand the concept. In general, people know very well what it means to be overwhelmed, how it feels, and what we intuitively do to overcome this state. They also have a great grasp of how it feels to flourish, especially in their work lives. But the gap between these two states nonetheless looms large for most of us.

There's a lot we can learn and do beyond this basic knowledge. So let's explore what being overwhelmed involves in a bit more detail.

General Adaptation Syndrome and the Stress Curve

General adaptation syndrome—the predictable stages involved in the stress response—was first described by the Hungarian Canadian endocrinologist Hans Selye in 1936. His research focused on the physiological changes we experience when undergoing different levels of intensity of this crucial physiological mechanism. Specifically, Selye's work delved into the adaptive capacities of our bodies, and how those capacities can backfire under certain conditions, resulting in a maladaptive cycle.

But Selye was not the first to describe the effects of the physiological response we call stress, although he is considered the father of this concept in our era. Hippocrates, twenty-four centuries ago, described something very similar to our contemporary concept of stress: our characteristic bodily response that allows us to fight against any disease and to restore normalcy. He called this condition *ponos* (toil).

Both Hippocrates and Selye knew that our complex, amazing bodies deploy a range of tools to maximize our chances of survival. One of the consequences of our current 24/7 on-duty/at-work lifestyle is that these tools begin to overperform—and we thus start losing a basic awareness of our internal energy level. In other words, because we're always preoccupied with being busy, we've relegated the perception of our fundamental physiological needs to the sidelines. We no longer have a good sense of when it's time to stop and recharge our batteries.

Nonetheless, we do have important insights that can mitigate this sorry state. For one, we have an ever-deepening comprehension of how our bodies and minds react to different levels of stress—and how that impacts our actions.

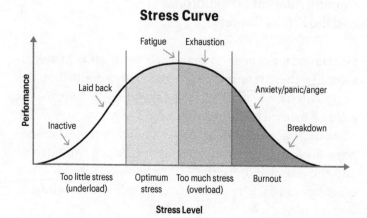

Stress Curve

This chart, based on Selye's pioneering work, shows the relationship between performance and stress level. Remember that we are talking about the real definition of stress, that is, the healthy bodily processes that facilitate the basic conditions of our daily lives. The four different sections of the arc represent the range of possible stress-performance correlations. When our stress level is too low, we are not able to function. This results in a nonexistent or low level of performance. The second area shows the optimum stress level needed to perform at our best. If we remain unaware of increasing levels of stress, we can inadvertently move to the third area. Here, even though our performance might still be high, our efforts come at the expense of intense physical and mental exertion. We may well become exhausted. If we are unable at this point to stop and take a break—a very common pattern in our lives—we typically progress into the final zone, where the risk of burnout is high and the performance level very low.

The higher stress zones encompass the final stage of general adaptation syndrome, in which our bodies have attempted to implement our stress response as a healthy, protective measure. This stage becomes entrenched when we ignore the body's valiant efforts to protect us from our own endless exertion, resulting in a natural decline in our mental and physical state.

The BRAC System

Let's bring in another component of this intricate and compelling puzzle. The BRAC (basic rest and activity cycle) system is another lens through which we can more deeply examine how our body integrates external influences.

BRAC: Basic Rest and Activity Cycle

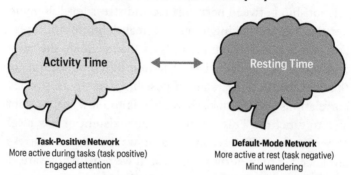

Task-Positive Network
More active during tasks (task positive)
Engaged attention

Default-Mode Network
More active at rest (task negative)
Mind wandering

Every day, our five brains—that is, our triune brains (which also encompass the two hemispheres explored in Chapter 1), plus our heart and gut brains—follow this cycle multiple times. Both elements of this cycle are very familiar to us, and, on some level, most of us realize that we need to alternate between them. But we certainly do not always do so in the most effective or healthy ways.

We are in an "activity" cycle in those moments during the day when we are focusing on a task, paying full attention to something, concentrating on an activity. We know today that the brain has several well-defined networks, each of which may or may not be activated, depending on our state of mind. The one that is turned on when we are in activity mode is called the task-positive network. This neural pathway is mainly located in our prefrontal cortex, which comprises our rational brain functions.

"Rest" time refers to those moments when our mind is wandering or daydreaming—when we think that we are doing nothing. These days, we know that in such states we are actually doing the opposite of nothing. Yet we continue to behave as if we've never learned the value of these seemingly quiet periods.

What do we normally do when we feel overwhelmed in our work? We sacrifice those moments we have for resting in favor of working more. We assume, incorrectly, that there are no consequences for resting less, and that we will keep being productive without a break. At the very least, we reckon that we will be able to produce and deliver more, at the expense of any resting time, of course.

Are we correct about all that productivity? The answer is an emphatic *no*. The problem, most of the time, is that we don't take into account the true significance of resting time when it comes to our brains. In other words, our incorrect assumption that we are doing nothing during rest times has led to habits that cause even further deterioration in our physical and mental condition.

Recent information from neuroimaging technologies reveals that those times when we think we're doing nothing are in fact the periods when our brain is working hardest of all. When our mind is at rest, as when we are daydreaming or just quietly sitting in a chair, there is a huge surge of activity in our brain. In this state, the brain activates a different neural pathway, known as the default-mode network. This pathway is more dispersed than the previous one and involves various cerebral structures beyond the cortical brain. Nowadays, we know that, during so-called resting times, the brain keeps consuming the same amount of energy as when it is active. We know that normally, our brain demands 20 percent of our resting metabolic rate (RMR)—the total amount of energy our bodies expend in one very lazy day of no activity. Its high rate of metabolism is remarkably constant despite widely varying mental and motoric activity.

That's fuel for vital brain activity, according to noted neurologists Marcus Raichle and Abraham Snyder. "A great deal of meaningful activity is occurring in the brain when a person is sitting back and doing nothing at all," Raichle, Snyder, and colleagues write. "It turns out that when your mind is at rest, dispersed brain areas are chattering away to one another."

One way to frame these findings is to see that famous "resting time" as a period during which the brain is performing an activity that's equivalent to what a computer does when we press the "save" button. We could say that the brain is putting our backup data in storage, analyzing all the inputs we constantly receive from the external world, and defining which ones are important for our life and which are not. At the same time, it's also distributing and organizing all of that information and all of our experiences into different "files" in our brain.

When we don't let our brain perform this task properly, our capacity for attention and performance during the activity part of the BRAC system is affected. When we force our brain to keep working—that is, by repeatedly choosing activity time over resting time—the brain will push back. It will, in effect, try to recover its resting time. The brain knows that it needs to do this job.

In these situations, the brain is basically being forced to perform both activities at the same time. In that context, it will prioritize data backup. We can recognize when this is happening—those all-too-common moments when we feel we are not able to focus or keep our attention on tasks. When we read the same sentence over and over.

Does this happen to you? I'll wager it does. We pretend that we are working, and we might even truly believe that we are ceaselessly working, but we are not.

It makes me laugh when someone tells me they worked on a cognition-oriented, sit-down project for ten hours straight. The truth is, that person might have been sitting in front of the computer for ten hours, but they were not really working the whole time. The brain simply cannot remain in activity/ task-positive mode for that long. It needs those breaks—and it will create them if you don't.

When we respect our need for resting time during the day, we gain the ability to recharge, and, in turn, we generate the potential to be substantially more productive. To be clear, I'm not referring here to sleeping time. I'm talking about those periods during the day when our mind is wandering and apparently unfocused, not when we are actually asleep. In a later chapter, we'll delve into how much rest time we need over the course of each day to keep being productive and even enhance our capacities. For now, let's take a closer look at our rest and activity cycles and their related neural pathways.

The following chart outlines the main features of these two key networks in our brain:

Task-Positive Network (TPN)	Default-Mode Network (DMN)
Focusing on a task	Dreaming
Actively paying attention (to something external)	Envisioning the future
Goal-orientation	Long-term memory
Reacting to, and working with, sensory information	Gauging others' perspectives
Short-term (working) memory	Theory of mind (understanding others)
Planning	Introspection
Abstract reasoning	Self-referential thought
The TPN is concentrated in the rational brain	**The DMN is widely dispersed throughout the brain**

Now that we've discussed both our natural and human-driven daily cycles of activity and resting time, let's use what we've learned to analyze a very popular misunderstanding in the business world: the idea that we can manage time. While we're at it, we'll investigate two science-backed explanations of how our natural physiological rest and activity cycles affect our lives. Then we'll look into ways we can use a better understanding of how time and energy are connected to maximize our potential.

Chronobiology and Time Management

We are always talking about how to design better approaches to "time management." There are tons of training courses and materials about this concept on the market. Anyone who's worked in any company long enough has probably received some kind of training in the subject. Throughout these endeavors, there's always an underlying feeling that time is a very scarce asset, a precious element in our lives. This perception is correct, but it's just a perception—and the way we approach it is wrong. It's not really the concept of time we need to focus on.

From my perspective, time management is the wrong target. Time is an immutable factor in the calculation of our existence here on earth. It's the most fixed element in our life equation. It will never change. It's a conventional agreement that applies, in the very same way, all around the world.

The right target, in my opinion, is good "energy management." What we are in charge of—in stark contrast with our utter lack of power over time—is how we deal with our energy. When we are tired, low in energy, we can rest; when we feel lively and energized, we can do more. In other words, we want to achieve allostasis, which occurs via smart "body budgeting." We each have a certain amount of energy, and we need to learn how to administer it properly.

We all tend to feel more or less productive over the course of the day. At any given moment, our state depends on a variety of parameters, including our level of motivation, previous activities, external pressures, feelings (enthusiasm, boredom, apprehension, and so on), even elements as simple but impactful as the time of day. In other words, how we feel—and function—depends directly on the level of energy we have.

And here is the fascinating part: our perception of time literally changes based on how we manage that energy level. If we've pushed ourselves to overdo it and find ourselves overwhelmed and unable to focus because our brain is trying to perform its rest duties, we think time is flying by with little getting done. On the other hand, when we are in a state of flow, passionately focused on a fulfilling activity, our perception of time passing seems to vanish. But time keeps running at its own pace in either case; it's just our minds that imagine otherwise.

Another general misunderstanding is the belief that our usage and reserves of energy progress in a linear fashion. This notion holds that we start the day with a large amount of energy, spend this energy during the day, and end up with a minimum amount of remaining energy as we head toward bed. However, it's a little more complicated than that.

The scientific study of the intersection of time and physical entities is known as chronobiology. Findings from this field can help us better understand how energy really works in our bodies—specifically, by looking into the two basic, day-to-day physiological rhythms all human beings possess, and that show that we are, in essence, "oscillatory beings."

Our Daily Cycles

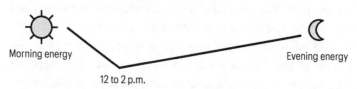

Morning energy

12 to 2 p.m.

Evening energy

Circadian Rhythm

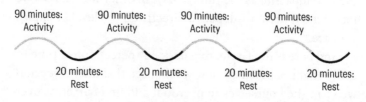

90 minutes: Activity   90 minutes: Activity   90 minutes: Activity   90 minutes: Activity

20 minutes: Rest   20 minutes: Rest   20 minutes: Rest   20 minutes: Rest

Ultradian Rhythm

The first of these two is our circadian rhythm. In a traditional model of this concept, we are thought to wake up with a large amount of energy (actually, not all of us do, as I will soon explain), consume a large proportion of that energy during the morning, reach our lowest level of energy between 12 and 2 p.m. (when basing the model on our typical daily working hours), and then somehow recover enough energy to allow us to be active for the rest of the day.

In medicine, we are very familiar with the low valleys of the circadian rhythm, when energy levels in the body are depleted. They are such a fundamental aspect of our existence, so real, that there is actually a higher incidence of medical issues, such as heart attack, strokes, and even death, between 3 and 5 a.m. (the nighttime equivalent of our midday slump) and during those two hours around noon. Don't panic, it's just a statistic!

Let's return to that moment around noon when we reach our lowest level of energy. More than thirty years ago, the *American Journal of Cardiology* sparked a veritable workplace revolution with its discussions of the impact of taking twenty-minute post-lunch breaks in the work environment. These ideas were based on findings initially published by the research journal *Sleep* in 1987. The original study showed profound benefits, as measured through a range of cardiac parameters, for those who participated in this rest time. Even more striking, the researchers concluded that those fifteen to twenty minutes (no more than twenty!) were not only enough to protect our heart from a range of complications, they actually boosted employees' energy, productivity, and motivation for the entire rest of the day! Those brief periods of downtime were so invigorating, it was almost like having two days in one.

This article greatly impressed the business world, especially in the United States. Many corporations started designing special rooms in the workplace where employees could rest for twenty minutes after lunch.

In those days, I was still living and practicing medicine in Argentina, and my medical colleagues and I were laughing our heads off over these "revelations." *Well*, we would joke, *finally the first world discovers the benefits of "la siesta!"*

In 2019, Tork, a leading global brand in workplace hygiene, conducted a survey to evaluate the impact of the loss of lunch breaks on Millennials. They concluded that "Millennials, who make up the largest generation in the U.S. workforce, feel more pressure to not take a lunch break than their Gen X and Baby Boomer counterparts, impacting their productivity, engagement and job satisfaction." Very interesting indeed: even though these findings don't specifically refer to the concept of taking a nap after lunch, they have a similar spirit, encompassing the need to take some form of rest in the middle of the day.

Many studies have resulted in similar findings on the benefits of naps, including one out of NASA connecting naps with improved working memory in astronauts. The study revealed that naps can:

- Boost memory and information retention five-fold
- Reduce stress and anxiety
- Improve cognitive function and creativity
- Reverse the productivity-destroying effects of a poor night's rest
- Beat caffeine for improving performance

Given these wonderful advantages, many well-known companies—including Google, PwC, Ben & Jerry's, Cisco, Zappos, Nike, Uber, White & Case, and Thrive Global—now support nap-taking in the workplace. These organizations know that enabling employees to nap during their low energy period is great for business.

So, what's your low energy period? Do we all share the same exact cycles? It turns out that, while we share certain aspects, our circadian rhythms do vary.

There are three general patterns of daily energy distribution. One group includes those we call "early birds" or "larks." Individuals with this type of rhythm are energized from the moment they wake up, feeling full of energy and highly aware. Early birds tend to lose energy as the day goes on and, quite naturally, prefer to go to bed on the earlier side. The second group are those (like me) who are "night owls," whose most energetic time of day is afternoons and evenings. Night owls experience their highest level of awareness later in the day, sometimes in the wee hours when most people are asleep.

The majority of people, however, experience the third pattern of daily energy cycle. This circadian rhythm is associated with two peaks of energy during the day: one in the morning and another in the afternoon/evening. People in this group are called "hummingbirds."

Why is this information important? Being aware of our own natural rhythms can help us leverage our daily energy peaks in much more productive ways. Let's say you need to work on a task that requires a large amount of energy, accuracy, concentration, and focus, and you are running out of time. The wisest thing to do under such circumstances is to proactively plan to get that job done during your highest peak of energy. That's what I do in my working life.

This chronobiological information is so important that the 2017 Nobel Prize in Physiology or Medicine was awarded to three researchers—Jeffrey Hall, Michael Rosbash, and Michael Young—whose work focused on circadian rhythms. Hall, Rosbash, and Young discovered that every single cell in our body has an internal clock that is aligned with our circadian rhythm. These clocks work together as a whole to help shape all aspects of human physiology. The researchers revealed many amazing ways in which our internal clocks and biological rhythms govern our lives. They also found that *all* living organisms on our planet operate on a twenty-four-hour cycle, in tune with the earth's revolution. Their work has been crucial to our understanding of how the light emanating from computers (and other screens) can affect our well-being as it takes us further and further out of sync with our internal timekeepers.

The second key energy pattern is called the ultradian rhythm: this is a natural physiological phenomenon that is not only intimately connected to our BRACs but also explains the alternations found in those cycles. This shorter sequence is also known as the 90/20 cycle. About every ninety minutes to two hours, the brain will "switch off" for around fifteen to twenty minutes—at least in terms of work-related tasks: during this time, the brain focuses its efforts on tasks unconnected to the outside world.

In an ideal world, these times of "rest" between periods of focused work would be convenient. In our busy real world, they're harder to accept, but—in some ways, sometimes—we naturally follow this pattern without realizing we are doing so.

We come to work early in the morning. A couple of hours later, we go for a coffee or a snack. Then, two hours later, it's lunch. Most of the time, we take another short break in the middle of the afternoon, even if it's just to walk to the watercooler or bathroom. These breaks are not happening by chance. Our inner body's rhythm is leading the way.

At the same time, it's also true that we break this cycle again and again due to meetings and deadlines, not to mention the ubiquitous pressures and burdens we face on the job. In such situations, we need to bear in mind that we pay a steep price when we consistently sacrifice rest due to work pressures.

After all, there is a counterintuitive outcome when we actually make the effort to mindfully adhere to our natural break-heavy rhythm. The main impact is that we increase our effectiveness! It is, quite simply, the easiest and fastest way to become more productive.

THE 100-MINUTE ALARM

In my programs, I tell the executives I work with to set an alarm to ring every ninety to 100 minutes, and, when it goes off, to stop whatever they're doing and shift to another activity for fifteen to twenty minutes. It's not always feasible in their work environment to spend time doing nothing at the end of each cycle, but there are other ways to address this deep biological need. For instance, I often suggest leveraging this time to perform easier or lighter tasks, such as answering uncomplicated emails, making low-key phone calls, talking to a colleague, or organizing their desk or home screen. Of course, going for a walk or simply resting will also help the brain do what it has to do. Bottom line, almost any clear-cut change in what you're doing can allow the brain a bit of a break.

EXERCISE: Adapting to the 90/20 Cycle

Remember what we discussed about resting time in this chapter: this seemingly inactive state allows the brain to do its most essential and hardest work—storing information, organizing its "files," performing imperative "backup information storage" processes. A simple change in activity, doing something that requires less focus or that enables a more relaxed perspective, helps the brain to do this indispensable work.

So, give it a try: use your tech to support your brain's health by setting two alerts on your phone (tip: use a ringtone that doesn't "stress you out"). Work in cycles of roughly 100 minutes on one task, and then fifteen to twenty on another (or take a break, if possible). You'll be amazed at how much more you can get done, while also experiencing less tension overall.

Once you've followed this rhythm for a couple of weeks, your brain may not even need to be reminded anymore. Moreover, you'll likely experience an exponential increase in effectiveness and productivity! This is not magic—it's just how the brain works. When you establish habits that are in accord with your chronobiological rhythms, you'll feel better, increase your focus and energy, and get more done.

Flourishing at Work:
The Thriving Formula

NOW THAT we've explored our relationship with stress and our basic physiological rhythms, I'm going to share eight practical tips for dealing with our chronically overwhelmed states of mind. Each of these tips is related to making the shift from that overwhelmed state to a flourishing way of being, and each includes a tool that will allow you to experience this science in action. Together, these eight techniques comprise my Thriving Formula, and they will help you incorporate brain-healthy, anti-tension habits into your daily life.

During my workshops, my participants often tell me about coping techniques they use, all of which typically touch on important elements of making the shift from overwhelmed to flourishing. My system is designed to combine these types of approaches in the most effective ways. Above all, it is imperative to practice each tip regularly over time if you want to receive the full benefit.

Tip 1: Overcome Anxiety

Anxiety is the most impactful manifestation of being over-whelmed, or at least the one that is mentioned most com-monly by people in leadership roles. It often seems like this problematic aspect of the overwhelmed state is everywhere, and it is being expressed in many different ways. But we've recently learned that anxiety has a unique characteristic, one that offers a lens into ways we may be able to escape this ostensibly inevitable, pervasive, and inexhaustible burden. Most people aren't aware of this characteristic, probably because it's really new information.

Here's the deal: anxiety can only manifest when our mind is connected with the past or with the future. On the one hand, we worry over *things that have already happened*. We may be anxious because we did not accomplish what we were supposed to do, or we had a meeting that didn't go well, or we didn't meet a deadline, or we had an unpleasant dis-cussion with our boss or a colleague, and so forth. If you're wondering how this helps us, rest assured: it doesn't.

On the other hand, we get anxious wondering about—and perseverating on—how to deal with potentially overwhelming scenarios that *might possibly occur* in conceivable future situ-ations. We might not be able to accomplish what we need to do, our meeting might not go well, we might not meet a dead-line... get the idea? We think we are working out solutions when in fact we are going around in circles worrying about things that will probably never happen. Again: not helpful.

The fantastic revelation we have today is this: anxiety quite simply cannot be present when we *keep our mind in the present*. The instant our mind jumps to the past or the future, we open the door for anxiety. When we are able to stay in the present moment, in the here and now, we can shut the door to anxiety. Thus, any technique that can help us keep our mind in the present moment can significantly reduce anxiety. Many such tools do already exist. For instance, most mindfulness practices are geared toward being attentive to the moment at hand. What's more, after forty years of use as a therapeutic tool for different medical conditions, mindfulness training has actually become a mainstream phenomenon in many organizations.

For our purposes, I'm proposing a slightly different technique, one that's traditionally used with patients who are dealing with phobias. All phobias have the same pattern: phobic symptoms appear because the person who suffers from the phobia is remembering an old, traumatic experience from the past. The main root of any phobia—neatly encompassing both poles of anxiety—is the fear that the same *past* situation could happen again in the *future*.

Tool: Being Present through Your Five Senses

The technique I have found most effective for addressing anxiety involves a practice that's sometimes called the "Rule of Five." You can also find it described as the "5-4-3-2-1 coping technique for anxiety." It's a very proactive, deceptively simple exercise that's grounded in our five senses. This is the reason I personally like it so much—it's practical, brief, effective, and can be practiced anytime, anywhere, as many times as you need. Here's how it works.

STEP 1: The very instant that you notice you are feeling anxious, stop doing whatever activity you are involved in at that moment and start anchoring your mind to the here and now. How do you do this? By paying attention to, recognizing, and naming your sensory experience in your current environment. If you are alone, practice this exercise out loud—it's more effective that way. When that's not possible, it's fine to just speak to yourself in a very low voice or even name things in silence, speaking the words in your mind.

5 SEE
4 FEEL
3 HEAR
2 SMELL
1 TASTE

STEP 2: <u>Begin with your sight.</u> Acknowledge <u>five different objects that you are able to see</u> around you in that place, in that moment. Then, move on to touch by noticing <u>four different elements that are physically in contact with you.</u> Continue by recognizing and naming <u>three sounds</u> you hear in your surroundings, then <u>two things you can smell.</u> Finally, acknowledge <u>one taste you are experiencing.</u>

STEP 3: Repeat this exercise as many times as you need to. It's very easy to integrate into your day, and, as you continue to explore the practice, you'll be improving your ability to be present in your daily life while boosting the positive effects of the exercise itself. Any moment that our mind can be anchored in the present means a moment when the symptoms of anxiety cannot manifest. In other words, <u>when we focus on the present, anxiety vanishes.</u> Again, it's not magic: it's how the brain works.

When we are able to <u>keep our mind in the present</u> time—here, by using tools that rely on a genuine scientific foundation—<u>there is literally no room for anxiety.</u> And remember, I'm using the word "moment." If you're too busy to go through all five senses or you feel more comfortable covering just the first few, that's totally fine. Sometimes I even stick with the first sense (sight), and that's enough for me to keep my control and stay centered in where/when I am.

Tip 2: Develop Awareness and Acceptance

Do you know how to boil a frog? When I ask my audiences this question, after the usual surprise and funny comments, somebody in the audience usually comes forward with the answer I'm looking for. For those of you who don't know, the allegory goes like this: Place the frog in a pot of cold water. Then, start to very gradually heat up that water. The frog cannot sense this slow and subtle change of temperature. Once the water is boiling, it's too late for the frog to react and try to escape.

[handwritten margin note: GRADUAL CHANGE IS IMPERCEPTIBLE]

I like to use this story because it is an excellent metaphor for what happens to us in the process of getting overwhelmed. We start our working day with our own to-do list. Even at this stage, we typically already have plenty of tasks to get through—and we don't know if we will be able to accomplish them all. When we arrive at work, we're faced with more to-dos! First, our colleague informs us that there is an urgent meeting that we didn't know about but must participate in. A bit later, our boss calls us in to discuss another project, something that was not on our original list. And, by the way, the first draft of that project must be turned in today. We can't say no to any of these obligatory requests. And we keep adding more and more tasks, both because we know they are important, and because we believe that we should, and can, accomplish them.

Somewhere in the course of days like this (for most of us, that means every day), we unknowingly cross the line from a healthy level of *stress* to an unhealthy state of *distress*. We're usually not aware of the moment when it all becomes "too much." At that point, our productivity starts suffering, and we start needing much more energy to perform the same tasks. We also start to sacrifice any time we might have used for resting or doing something revitalizing, because we "have

[handwritten margin note: HEAVY STRESS CAN BECOME UNHEALTHY WHEN WE DON'T GIVE NOTICE.]

If you fail to rest you can't perform your best.

to get things done." We tell ourselves we will rest when we finish ... *someday*. Day after day, we follow this same pattern, until *someday* becomes *never*.

This, dear reader, is how we've turned into a bunch of boiled frogs. The water starts warming up around us, and, because of our nonstop lives, we don't realize things are getting hotter and hotter. When we do finally take stock, it's too late.

super from Dan. From Dan.

Like frogs, when we're not able to stop in time, we end up in boiling water—and before we know it we're already cooked. Or, more precisely, *burned out*.

This is why it is so important to know ourselves well enough to understand when it's time to stop and recharge our batteries. Being aware of getting overwhelmed is not enough. When I'm leading a workshop that includes this theme, I always ask participants two questions. First, I ask whether they are aware of when they are overwhelmed, and with what level of accuracy they can recognize that state in themselves. Usually, almost everybody says they are aware, and that they feel fairly accurate in that assessment. Then I pose a revealing second question: What do you normally do in that moment? For this one, the response is almost always one of two things: "I keep working" or "I go for a coffee to gain some energy to keep working."

Clearly, recognizing when we are getting overwhelmed doesn't lead us out of hot water. We need to accept that we are prone to pushing ourselves to the point that we are in an unacceptable state, and we need to acknowledge just how unproductive and destructive that state is. Finally, we need to understand that it's time to stop contributing to our own overwhelmed condition. Long before we get too close to burnout, if possible.

For top-echelon employees and employers, the idea that we sometimes need to stop working can seem, on the surface, ludicrous. But it's as undeniable as any scientific fact. So, especially for people who see themselves as "driven," "competitive," and "high-achieving," acceptance is a huge component of this process. Only when we accept our state— and comprehend the causes thereof—can we make a change. As Carl Jung used to say: "What we resist persists." Trust me, *WHAT WE* denial is a bad counselor. Acceptance, on the other hand, is *DON'T CHANGE* a conduit to solutions. *REMAINS*

Tool: Practice Awareness

When we are overwhelmed, there is only one thing that works: taking time out and resting. Here's something incredibly simple I want you to try—a practice that represents a small yet significant step toward both awareness and acceptance. It's also an incremental way to get back on track with your BRACs (basic rest and activity cycles), by beginning to integrate some rest throughout your activities and allowing the brain a backup period, however brief.

STEP 1: Take a small piece of paper. An index card is perfect. On one side, write the word "overwhelmed"; on the other, write "resting." Place it in a spot close to your computer, or wherever you spend most of your work hours, with the "overwhelmed" side facing up. Each time that word catches your eye, pause for a second and notice any feelings of being overwhelmed. Then, turn the paper over and "rest." Maybe it's only for the space of one long, deep breath, but, during that single breath, close your eyes and really release your thoughts, and relax your jaw, shoulders, and so on. (Of course, a longer break is good, too.) This helps your vagus nerve reestablish equilibrium and equanimity. Then turn the paper back over and proceed with your work.

STEP 2: Over time, move the paper around once in a while, and maybe even switch between a couple of note cards in different colors and sizes, so your brain doesn't get habituated to the same old reminder. You can also get creative on this one—paint the words or related symbols on a flat rock or use something else that will resonate with your brain and help you gain mindfulness in this way. You might even consider sharing this practice with your team, thereby encouraging them to nurture their best and most productive selves.

Tip 3: Balance Your Energy

When we are overwhelmed, what we need most is energy. Therefore, it's very important to have a clear understanding of two related skills: how we can increase our energy stores and how we can avoid draining them, especially when it's time to conserve resources.

Let's explore a very old technique, one that has been used for thousands of years, in various iterations, in Indigenous communities all over the world. An energy balance chart is an ancient art that is of paramount usefulness in our busy modern times. I highly recommend that all my clients take the time and care to build this chart—and keep it updated, too. This efficient tool works by enabling you to assess your energetic profile, including what builds you up and what depletes you on an energetic level.

Tool: The Energy Balance Chart

This exercise helps us become more explicitly conscious of what we can do—or avoid doing—to balance our energy. If feeling overwhelmed is a consequence of low energy, reflecting on and increasing your exposure to the elements in your life that boost energy, counter overwhelm, and allow you to flourish is a super-savvy move.

STEP 1: Draw a chart with four columns and four rows. In the first column, leave the first row blank and then write "people," "places," and "activities" in the next three spaces (top to bottom). At the top of the second column, write "energy sources," then "energy drains," then "mixed."

	Energy Sources	Energy Drains	Mixed
People			
Places			
Activities			

STEP 2: Now, take your time and identify those people, places, and activities that are energy sources for you. How do you know they are energy sources? It's very simple. Energy sources are those people, places, and activities that make you feel good. Feeling good is a physical manifestation of gaining energy. Find as many energy sources as you can in each category. Please don't filter your selection process with notions of who or what "should" be on your list, just go with your gut (brain). You'll probably want to start with the space at the intersection of energy sources and people. Perhaps the people on your list are not necessarily the ones you'd expect. Maybe they are not even part of your family or friend group. Don't worry about it—that's actually the case for most of us! In my workshops, I always ask the audience to give me specific examples from their lives, and their lists almost always include someone who's not a close friend or relative.

STEP 3: In the next row, write down the places that give you a good feeling when you visit them. This should feel pretty easy. My audiences often mention certain parks, coffee shops, churches, different parts of the city they live in, a friend's house, a favorite area in their own home, and so on.

STEP 4: In the last row of the second column, list those activities that raise your energy. Here, people often refer to playing a sport, going to the gym, or some other athletic activity, such as running. Walking the dog is always very popular, as are reading, listening to music, and playing an instrument. Video games are also highly rated. I don't recall anybody ever mentioning watching TV in this category. While that can be a relaxing activity, it's not necessarily one that will help us raise our energy. Cooking, cleaning the house, and other domestic tasks are sometimes included in this space.

STEP 5: Now, do the same process for your energy drains. In this section, we identify those people, places, and activities that deplete our energy. We don't feel good when we go to certain places, do certain activities, or spend time around certain people. As you did for energy sources, take your time thoughtfully filling out each category, trying not to filter your responses. Yes, you will sometimes find that your answers are not quite what you might expect or prefer.

STEP 6: The last column, labeled "mixed," is for those people, places, and activities that are neither entirely drains nor sources of energy. They may have been energy sources for a while, and then became energy drains. Or perhaps they are sometimes nourishing to your energy, and other times more depleting or destructive. List these as well, as honestly as possible, bearing in mind that such entities have a potentially ambiguous effect on your energy.

STEP 7: Your energy balance chart may change significantly over time, so this is a good exercise to repeat on a regular basis.

Tip 4: Change the Meaning

Albert Ellis, a psychologist and the creator of Rational Emotive Behavior Therapy (REBT), developed another therapeutic tool known as the ABC model. In essence, Ellis's ABC approach offers a different, more constructive way to understand the impact of our life experiences.

In his model, the "A" stands for adversity, or the activating event; and "C" refers to consequences. We generally believe that the consequences of any event are a natural outcome of the event itself, as well as of the adversity associated with that event. Ellis claims that this conception is wrong. In his view, any consequence associated with any event is not a direct consequence of that event, or even of the adversity it entailed. He argues that the consequences of any given event in truth depend on a completely different factor: "B," or our beliefs. That is, the way an event affects us results almost entirely from the way we understand the event.

The ABC Model	
A	Adversity/Activating Event
B	Beliefs
C	Consequences

Ellis found that the same event could affect different people in totally different ways. We create narratives based on our beliefs, and the meaning we give to any event is connected with our own story, our own experiences. Thus, our understanding of any event fundamentally depends on our past experiences. Therefore, a positive or negative impact doesn't depend on the event, but on how it interacts with our own story.

The way we frame events is another area that is ripe for evolution in each of us. We can use what we know about our brain to learn new skills that help us amplify and reinforce actions and neural pathways that allow us to flourish; here, we can do so by telling ourselves healthier stories.

We need to understand and take care of what we believe. As author and relationship expert Lisa Hayes wrote, "Be careful how you are talking to yourself, because you are listening."

Tool: Your ABC Model

Remember, the past is just a story we tell ourselves. If we change the story, we change its emotional impact on us. And we *can* change our story—in other words, the way we understand an event. If you think about it, this process is something we go through many times in our lives. Say you get your heart broken (adversity/activating event) and, as a consequence, you come to believe a very sad story about yourself and your romantic life. Some time later, you meet the love of your life. Now, you believe that your earlier heartbreak was all for the best. You're grateful for something that once seemed unbearable. Same event, different beliefs. Sound familiar? It happens all the time. We just don't usually look at our lives from the ABC perspective.

Let's try doing so now. We'll approach our ABC models from two angles.

STEP 1: First, take a few minutes to think about an activating event in your life that you initially viewed as negative, but later considered to be positive. Your perception may have changed because you gained the wisdom to tell yourself a bigger story, or because you eventually saw a concrete positive outcome. If it helps to write your thoughts down, by all means do so. In any case, note that the original event remains unchanged. The consequence, however, shifted—according to your beliefs.

STEP 2: Now, bring to mind something from the past that still holds adversity for you. Can you find a way to look at that event differently? It might be that you can find a silver lining, a good result; perhaps you are able to have a broader perspective, and not take things personally; or maybe you just don't want to indulge in negative self-talk about it anymore.

The consequence of this exercise is that we begin to understand that we have the power to change the emotional impact of any negative event in our lives. When we change the meaning of the stories in our brain, we literally change our brain; in turn, we add a bit more momentum to our shift from overwhelmed to flourishing.

Tip 5: Explore Your Inner Physiological Cycles

When we identify and follow our inner physiological cycles, we enable ourselves to move away from time/energy management habits that don't serve us—and we progress toward our goal of thriving. We grow more in tune with ourselves from the cellular level on up to our most intricate system, our brains. So we definitely need to find out as much as we can about our own inner rhythms.

Tool: Honor Your Chronobiology

You probably already have a sense of your circadian rhythm, or chronotype, but these inner-rhythm exercises will allow you to become an expert on yourself. You'll find that respecting your chronobiological cycles will not only increase your productivity but also your quality of life overall. It might even give rise to ingenious ideas for improving your organization by integrating chronobiology into your workplace and management practices.

STEP 1: Take a few days to observe your particular manifestation of the circadian rhythm. Are you a lark, an owl, or a hummingbird? Whichever you decide, can you figure out just how much of that type you are? For example, if you're a lark, does your big energy moment occur in the morning in general, or very, very early, before most people are awake? If you're an owl, does that mean afternoons are good for you, or do you do your best thinking late at night? And if you're a hummingbird, do your optimal energy times occur in line with the average hummingbird, that is, morning and early evening (with a low in between), or are you a bit different?

STEP 2: Now that you've researched yourself, put your findings into action. Leverage your daily peak of energy by scheduling important tasks or meetings during your high energy periods. Try to find ways to support a flourishing mindset and decent productivity during your lower energy periods, too.

STEP 3: The next part of this exercise will help with both the peak and low phases of your cycle. First, let's look into how we can use what we know about our ultradian rhythms to reduce feelings of overwhelm in our lives. We have already discussed setting an alarm and changing to a lighter activity every 100 minutes or so (our cycles range from ninety to 120 minutes) while you are at work. Taking this a little further, I want you to practice the ultradian cycle for an entire day, so you'll probably need to initially try it over the weekend. Yes, I know, in this day and age, most of us work more or less every day of the week. But we usually have more leeway on weekend days, right? (If you don't, you definitely need to implement this entire formula, pronto!) The important thing is to take the full fifteen- to twenty-minute break *each time*. In fact, set a second alarm, to ensure your breaks are long enough—and while you're at it, make sure the ringtone is pleasant, not alarming. Since you're doing this on your own dime, make sure those breaks consist of something you find truly restful, such as lying in a hammock, taking a leisurely walk, enjoying a nice cup of tea or glass of wine, or playing with a pet.

Try to start the last exercise on a Saturday, because once you've authorized yourself to alternate periods of activity and rest, you'll probably want to try it on Sunday as well. The benefits will be so obvious that you'll be inspired to find innovative ways to follow this natural schedule all day at work as well. This step alone will gradually train your neurology to thrive.

Tip 6: Stop Multitasking

You're exhausted, sleepy, and totally lacking in energy, but you don't have any choice: You need to finish that project that's due today. You must prepare that other presentation for tomorrow. You need to finish your plan for your hundredth meeting that day, too. At the same time, you're always going for high-quality work and trying to be more productive, right? What can you do?

There is one very simple solution—however controversial— and I say it with all of my medical authority, because you will be reluctant to believe that it's true: stop multitasking!

First of all, our brain is not suited to multitasking. It cannot perform two tasks at the same time. Only the tiniest fraction of people on earth can even begin to successfully approximate something that we could call real multitasking. What we normally do is switch very quickly from one task to the next, a draining behavior known as context shifting. We move back and forth from one activity to another, but we are not really multitasking in the sense that we believe we are. Moreover, many studies have shown that our efforts to multitask are not only unsuccessful, they actually lead to other issues.

The negative consequences of multitasking are legion:

- **It reduces smaller gray-matter density in the anterior cingulate cortex:** This is the area that is involved in processing emotions and behavior regulation.

- **It leads to increased anxiety:** Neuroscientists say that multitasking literally drains your mind's energy reserves, causing you to lose focus and become more anxious.

- **It impacts your short-term memory:** A 2011 study out of the University of California, San Francisco, found that multitasking negatively impacts your working memory— your brain's "scratchpad," which it uses to manage and focus on key information.

- **It inhibits creative thinking:** The added anxiety and lack of brain "space" caused by multitasking can also cause you to lose your ability to think outside the box. To be creative, our minds need time to digest or "incubate" new ideas.

- **It stops you from getting into a state of flow:** Flow is the wonderful state of mind in which we're so focused on a task that our productivity skyrockets. In one example, executives said they were 500 percent more productive while in a state of flow! This invaluable way of working and being requires sustained effort and focus, two qualities that multitasking precludes.

- **It causes more mistakes and less productivity:** Multiple studies have shown that multitasking causes people to take longer to do simple tasks, reduces IQ by an average of ten points, and can even have a negative impact equivalent to losing a night of sleep.

We have a specific amount of mental energy as far as our level of attention, focus, and capacity for understanding. When we attempt to work on many tasks at the same time, our brain must distribute some of that finite energy to each activity. Therefore, every disparate task receives a smaller chunk of energy or attention—never enough to be at the peak of our productivity.

I know, I know, we cannot expect to stop being multitaskers. Nowadays, every job description insists that candidates should be effective multitaskers. Luckily, there is a counterintuitive solution to this dilemma. You see, usually, at the very moment we are running out of time and have too many things on our plate, our brain will start working in parallel, jumping from one task to the other. This is what we mistakenly call multitasking.

It turns out that what we need to do to maximize our potential when we have a low level of energy and pressing time constraints is to move to a linear way of working. By focusing our energy on one task at a time, we can avoid the many pitfalls of multitasking outlined above. If we feel that we are running out of energy and we need to finish many different tasks, we need to prioritize and then start solving one task after the other.

Tool: Linear Activity

Applying all of our remaining energy to just one activity at a time vastly increases our probability of getting an excellent result—whatever we are involved in. This exercise will help you allocate your energy in exactly this way the next time you find yourself panicking (hi there, reptilian brain!) over your to-do list.

STEP 1: Allow yourself the space for your rational brain (which can grasp the science behind the superiority of a linear approach) to take over. Acknowledge the perfectly reasonable overwhelmed feelings that arise when you have too many things to do and are running out of time, and then take a moment to focus on one thing: your priorities. List these in order of importance.

STEP 2: Next, address the first priority with your whole focus trained on that one thing. Once you have accomplished that priority to an adequate degree, that's when you can move on to doing the next thing. And the next.

You will get a million times more done in this way, I promise. And you'll be practicing a crucial facet of your journey to a flourishing life.

Tip 7: Implement Healthy Rituals

Before we discuss this tip, I am going to ask you to stop reading and write down a list of the rituals in your daily life. Take your time. Think carefully. Pay attention to your regular daily activities, as there is an overlap between rituals, habits, and routines. All refer to repetitive actions that have some meaning for us, such as the way we greet our partner, or the way we groom ourselves when we wake up.

Try this now. I'll wait.

OK, did you take your time on the list? How many rituals were you able to come up with? If you were thorough, you probably wrote down at least twenty. Maybe more. Our life is a continual series of rituals.

To some extent, rituals are not only a human characteristic—they exist in the animal kingdom as well. Rituals are everywhere. But *why* are they so omnipresent? And how do they impact our behavior?

Rituals are connected to what we sometimes call "the anxiety dial." That is, they act as a natural anxiolytic, or anxiety reducer. Rituals convince our brain that things in our world are predictable, ordered, and safe. They increase our sense of stability and continuity and are one of the central components of social health.

In this regard, rituals appeal to our rational, reptilian, and emotional brains, each of which craves predictability for different reasons. For all three, rituals represent safety. A predictable world is a safe world. If I know what is going to happen, I can be prepared to act—and, potentially, to defend and protect myself. The repetitive and stable aspects of rituals feel especially soothing to the reptilian brain.

But there is another component that mostly involves the emotional and rational brains: our identity. We express and affirm who we are through many different sources, with rituals being a very powerful aspect of how we do so: "This is the way I like my coffee," "I always do it in this way because it's more effective," "When I dress like this, I feel like myself," and so on. Then our multiple brains can say: "This is me; I recognize myself through these rituals."

For the rational brain, predictability also helps with making plans. Remember how the brain always needs a plan? In order to be prepared, the rational brain builds plans or strategies, incorporating rituals throughout, from list-making to routine actions. Meanwhile, the reptilian brain is always in reacting mode. In this planning-reacting context, the emotional brain acts as an umbrella, overarching and connecting the rational and reptilian realms. In essence, rituals allow these three brains to act as a team.

Rituals are also meaning-makers. They structure our lives and are inherently linked with our values. They express, in action, what we care about, what we believe matters.

Rituals are related to our survival. A successful *repeatable* strategy can make the difference between life and death on an evolutionary scale. Perhaps for this reason, the need for rituals is a basic human instinct, as real, as urgent, and as raw as our needs for food, shelter, and love.

As behavioral scientist Nick Hobson writes, "We agree that life is full of uncertainty, but the blooming, buzzing confusion of our world stands little chance against the power of rituals."

Now that we have a slightly better understanding of the importance of rituals, let's go to the next level. How many of those rituals on your list would you say are healthy for you? For instance, smoking can certainly calm your nerves, but we already know with 100 percent certainty that cigarettes lead to many physical illnesses and, often, death. The short-term effect of smoking is positive, but the middle- and long-term effects are definitely negative.

Let's evaluate our rituals and get those that are healthy for our lives on the front burner. We've got a fantastic neuroscience-based tool for this process—the law of the four Ps.

Tool: The Four Ps of Healthy Rituals

The brain cannot make big changes all at once. New Year's resolutions tend to fail because we are expecting too much from ourselves over a short period of time. We put the bar too high, push ourselves to jump over it immediately, and then give up. Remember: small steps, big changes. This exercise will help you take your current rituals and make them more positive and more useful.

STEP 1: First, consider the four Ps that make for healthy rituals:

- **Personal:** Your rituals should be related to you. They should be connected with your life, and with what is important to you.

- **Possible:** Your rituals must be realistic. They should entail something you can start doing today and keep doing for a long period of time.

- **Pragmatic:** Your rituals should be practical and simple.

- **Progressive:** Whether you are enacting a new ritual or leaning in on a great preexisting aspect of your life, make sure implementation is gradual and achievable.

STEP 2: Next, take a good look at the list of rituals you wrote at the beginning of this tip, keeping the four Ps in mind. Which rituals contribute to good moods and feelings, and allow you to shine at work or at home? You want to emphasize and encourage those pro-thriving rituals, habits, and routines that you can regularly implement.

STEP 3: Now, take some time to write down at least one new ritual that you think will help you in your daily life. Take

special care that any new idea meets the fourth criterion—
you don't want to be self-defeating here, or contribute to
feeling overwhelmed!

Whether checking over your list to see which rituals are
most beneficial or choosing a new healthy ritual, adhere to
the rule of the four Ps. With this exercise, your rituals—new
and old—will become increasingly positive and effective
over time.

Tip 8: Follow the PERMA Program

Martin Seligman, a longtime professor at the University of
Pennsylvania, is often called the father of positive psychology. A few years ago, the U.S. Army contacted Seligman
to discuss the possibility of developing a program that
would help their military personnel deal with a higher-than-
average incidence of psychological challenges, including
PTSD, depression, bipolar disorders, anxiety, and so on.

Seligman and his team created a program called PERMA,
which is currently being implemented with great success by
more than a million Army personnel. PERMA stands for:

- Positive emotions
- Engagement
- Relationships
- Meaning
- Accomplishment

Seligman's book *Flourish: A Visionary New Understanding
of Happiness and Well-Being* describes his system in detail.
Here, we're going to take a closer look at two elements of
Seligman's acronym: P, or positive emotions, and M, or

meaning. We'll unpack the ways these two qualities impact our state of mind and can help us move from an overwhelmed state to one in which we are truly flourishing.

Let's start with positive emotions. Seligman says that building up a store of positive emotions can produce a more enduring positive effect on how we feel than any mood-boosting medication. In other words, the positive impact of any emotion-modulating medication will last only as long as we are taking that medication. But, Seligman says, when we are able to produce positive emotions by ourselves, those feelings are like goods stored in a warehouse. We can go to that mental space and extract our positive emotions again and again.

But what do we mean by "positive"? It's very important to understand that this quality is not necessarily analogous to the concept of happiness. Being positive is a different state of mind. It doesn't mean that everything in your life is perfect. And it doesn't imply denial, either. It's merely an executive directive to focus on solutions rather than problems.

Another thing: being positive is not entirely about attitude. Let's say there is a very nice person on our team—someone who smiles most of the time, spreading good vibes. This person might be a great colleague, but all of those happy qualities don't necessarily add up to true positivity.

When we talk about being positive, we're talking about actions and facts. That person on our team who—when we are facing a challenge, a problem, a difficult task—is always the first to say, "Let's try it," "Let's do it," "Let's go for it," and "If it doesn't work we will try again"? That's the positive person.

When I bring this concept up during my presentations, participants very often share revealing stories about someone on their team who follows this pattern. Somebody who doesn't express their emotions very much, who may even be kind of a grumpy person. But every time something has to be done, this person is the first in line to offer their best efforts. Positivity, then, involves tangible effort.

So, it makes sense that Seligman's team also discovered that at least 50 percent of positive emotions are connected to physical activities. In other words, they found that positive interior emotions can be triggered by what we do on the outside. This means having a positive attitude or emotion may feel like something that naturally arises in the mind, yet it's actually often the other way around: physical activities can spur positive emotions that influence our mood. On one level, this is common knowledge: when you are not in your best mood, you go for a walk or go to the gym to get your endorphins going and enjoy a change of pace. But Seligman's work has bigger implications for any physical/exterior actions you might take.

Now let's take a look at meaning. Seligman's team had one group of people do something fun and asked another group to engage in a philanthropic activity. After the experience, both groups were asked about their emotions. The group that had practiced a fun activity reported that they had a great time, but their positive feelings didn't last very long after the event itself. The researchers found that the ensuing positive emotions lasted much longer in the philanthropic group.

This is a very interesting finding. We tend to think that philanthropy is something for a certain kind of person, someone selfless, someone who prioritizes helping others over their own needs. While it's true that serving those in need is "the right thing to do," it's also an activity that induces positive emotions in the giver that outlast any gained from fun. I like to say, "Be selfish, help others"—a phrase with more to it than we might expect, since activities with a larger meaning continue to resonate with us over the longer term.

Tool: The PERMA Program in Action

Positivity, a key component of the path to a flourishing life, is found in concrete, proactive behaviors. These actions are in turn linked with positive emotions. You might consciously feel or act happier, or you might not, but you'll be doing something that contributes to the shift we are seeking. Here are two steps you can take to bring more positivity into your day.

STEP 1: List some positive actions you've taken lately. Try to recall how you felt at the moment and afterward, bringing to mind both sense impressions of your outer environment and the positive emotions you felt inside at the time. Hold the memory in your mind, on all these levels and as long as you can, knowing that as you do so you are adding to the stores of your emotional warehouse.

STEP 2: As you move through your day, look for opportunities to practice real positivity via a solution orientation and tangible actions. When you find yourself flagging or feeling overwhelmed, try to get (pro)active right away or, if that's not possible, review a positive act in your mind, like you did in step I.

Likewise, these next two steps can also help you incorporate more meaning into your life by making a habit of regularly prioritizing the needs of others.

STEP 1: Think about minor times during your day when you might have to choose between mildly pleasurable altruism and highly enjoyable fun. While your instinct might be to go for the latter, notice what happens when you instead choose to do something selfless. You could even combine the two: the next time you head to the watercooler, invite someone on your team who seems a bit down or disconnected to join you. Or, spring for enough of your favorite snack to enjoy and share with your whole office.

STEP 2: Over time, as you consistently make choices like these, you'll reinforce those positive neural pathways and more frequently engage in the kinds of meaningful activities that have a lasting impact on your well-being.

It's Your Choice: Thermostat or a Thermometer?

We high achievers think we know a lot, don't we? But if you're reading this book, you're probably ready to accept that you've got more to learn. And that's a good thing.

Yes, we know that we want to shift from our position at the far end of the stress curve, the overwhelmed state, to one in which we are living in total wellness and functioning at our absolute best. We want to move beyond the reptilian brain's knee-jerk reactions to wise, meaningful, pro-health actions and states of mind. We want to align all of our brains and all of our natural cycles to optimize our productivity and relationships at work and beyond.

But we don't know how. In fact, much of the neuroscience on stress is profoundly counterintuitive, so we even have a hard time with the knowledge we do gain. Our rational brain is the engine of all of our technological advances and more, but it is not in charge of our survival instinct, which tells us to "Go! Go! Go!" when we should be resting. And it doesn't seem to be the most influential force in our highly competitive, nonstop business environments, either, which is why we—especially those of us in leadership roles—feel compelled to demonstrate our relentless devotion to the daily grind.

These are exactly the sort of detrimental, externally motivated impulses that my formula mitigates. I like to explain it through the following metaphor: the goal is to become a thermostat—and to avoid being a thermometer. A thermometer's temperature depends completely on its external environment. The function of a thermostat, on the other hand, is to use the tools at its disposal to keep the temperature at a set, optimal level. Which of the two is in control?

When we implement my Thriving Formula, we're seizing control by taking advantage of the latest science, combined with a dash of time-honored wisdom, to cultivate habits and practices that work. And we're doing so in ways that build upon each other in our brains, bodies, even our environments, so that we can see steady, measurable progress across the board.

Where will the evolution of our brain will take us next? It's hard to say, but each of us is working on it every day, in the ways we connect, think, learn, and grow. As we investigate and practice ways to better manage ourselves via our natural physiological responses and chronobiological cycles, we will also improve the ways we manage our relationships, teams, and more. Our prefrontal cortex, or rational brain, has yet to reach its full potential. But it can certainly lead us in this endeavor—with input from our heart and gut brains, too. You see, our five brains are connected, working together, and moving forward to a very promising, flourishing future.

THE THRIVING FORMULA: 8 TIPS TO FLOURISHING

TIP 1: Overcome Anxiety

Use all five of your senses to stay present in the current moment by employing the Rule of Five, otherwise known as the 5-4-3-2-1 coping technique for anxiety.

TIP 2: Develop Awareness and Acceptance

Use index cards and physical tokens to remind yourself to rest before you reach overwhelm.

TIP 3: Balance Your Energy

Gain awareness of your energy sources and energy drains by drafting up your own "energy balance chart" of people, places, and activities.

TIP 4: Change the Meaning

Use the ABC model—adversity/activating event, beliefs, and consequences—to reframe your thinking around challenging or activating events.

TIP 5: Explore Your Inner Physiological Cycles

Monitor your energy to discover your own circadian and ultradian (90/20) rhythms—and then honor your chronobiology by arranging your day around these natural cycles.

TIP 6: Stop Multitasking

However effective it may feel, multitasking does not work! Prioritize linear activity over working in parallel.

TIP 7: Implement Healthy Rituals

Remember your four Ps to design habits that will do you good: personal, possible, pragmatic, and progressive.

TIP 8: Follow the PERMA Program

Put the PERMA program into action by seeking meaning through philanthropy, and by always remembering that true positive emotions come from doing.

Train Your Brain to Tackle Organizational Transformation with Gusto

E'VE SPENT the last few chapters developing a holistic picture of how our brains work, as well as getting acquainted with practices that can optimize our neural functioning to improve our business acumen and more. Now, we're going to turn to more specific modalities in order to better manage what is arguably the most important element of sustained corporate success today: change.

In the business context, the word "change" has transcended its original definition to encompass an ever-larger range of processes. Internal programs, external courses and trainings, certifications in change management, change implementation specialists... You can literally find hundreds of millions of related results online. Given what's out there, you can apparently "change" just about anything in your company these days. There is even an international organization, the Association of Change Management Professionals, with thousands of members from all over the world. In fact, I was honored to be invited to present my workshop on the process of change in the brain at one of their annual conferences a couple of years ago.

When I find so many offerings, proposals, experts around a topic, there is a question that I always ask myself—and that's *why?* Some explanations are quite simple. Perhaps the notion of change represents a good business opportunity due to the high needs of the market. Or maybe it's because change does not seem to arise through easy solutions, and therefore companies end up hiring different providers, one after another, often undergoing repeated failures. In medicine, when an illness has too many treatments, we sometimes say all those options mean there isn't really any one good treatment available.

This leads us to another question: if we know that change is a constant—and never more so than in these new world circumstances—what are the real reasons why implementing change is so difficult?

Guess What? It's All about the Brain

We'll delve more deeply into the science behind how our brain—or, our five brains—reacts to change later, but for now, let's look a bit at how individuals and organizations think about change and the brain. When I give my seminars, I always start by asking the audience three questions:

1 What does change mean to you?
2 When you hear the word "change," what feelings come to mind?
3 How often do you experience change in your life?

Bringing up the concept of change always kicks off a lively debate, revealing many different attitudes among the participants. In the end, each person's contribution reflects a combination of how they feel about change and their own personality.

Audience members typically start by giving socially acceptable responses—remember that these conversations occur at the beginning of the seminar, when the climate for sharing more freely has not yet been created. Similarly, participants often give slightly glib answers to the second question, at least at the outset. When I insist on asking about the deeper feelings or emotions the word "change" elicits, the answers almost always lean in the same direction: anxiety, energy, opportunity, improvement, work, survival, uncertainty. In one word, fear.

Fear, fear, fear, fear.

The third question is admittedly a bit tricky. What I am actually interested in is observing the participants' unconscious reactions. Everyone rationally knows that change is a constant. However, we often hesitate to identify and accept this reality, and our default perception is one of a life full of monotony and repetition, devoid of change. I have to use a variety of approaches to help participants accept that—even in our apparently routine daily lives—changes are omnipresent.

This leads me to the underlying topic here, which is our brain's perception of change. What relationship exists between changes and our mind?

Your Brain Is Not Friends with Change

It's time to dive into the system that has evolved in our brain to resist change, the triggers to its activation, and the neural mechanisms we can lean on in order to overcome these barriers.

If we think about it in any depth, we all know that change is part of our daily life. We realize that we have a basic resistance to change, too. So, what does our brain do to resolve this bizarre duality? It's actually remarkably simple: it generates the illusion of permanency. Our brain creates a mental process that interprets our daily life as a series of repeated events.

Nothing is further from reality.

And it's not like we haven't known this for thousands of years. As Heraclitus (535–475 BCE) said, "Everything flows, nothing stands still." In other words: "The only constant in life is change."

Definitely a cliché, but a profoundly true one.

But remember—the brain has many ways of creating "realities," generating both internal processes and external actions that (it believes) will help us feel safe and in control. We cannot deny that this neurological propensity represents a logical, even to-be-expected self-protective mechanism, given that uncertainty is an awfully bad companion for our brain. Anything new or different or unknown makes our brain extremely nervous.

With change rampant on the corporate front, we see the impact of this natural neural response throughout organizations. Leaders who hope to get ahead of the curve need to gain a strong grasp of how the brain handles change. And that holds true for themselves as much as it does for their teams! That being said, let's dig a little deeper into the science behind the brain's reactivity to change.

To the brain, any uncertain situation implies potential danger. Why? The answer here is simple: If I do not know what's coming, I can't be prepared. Moreover, I can't know how to defend or protect myself.

So when it comes to the relationship between our brain and the process of change, we must ensure that we are at least one step ahead of our natural neurological responses. If those perceived change-related dangers and challenges arise from a lack of information, then perhaps we should stop focusing on the change itself. In fact, the big issue when dealing with change is related to the level of information we have at that time.

When I introduce this concept in my workshops, I pause to ask the audience another question: "Are any of you thinking or dreaming of a change in your life right now? Would you like to share it?" Not everyone does, and I respect their choice. But I nonetheless encourage each person to think about that dream, that change... and to consider what they feel when they do so. Never once has the word "fear" been included in the list of feelings shared in this context. Always, participants respond with positive emotions.

From there, I invite people to dive more profoundly into these dreams for a moment. Then, I start presenting potential options: changing jobs, earning more money, moving to a different place (whether quieter or more exciting), deeper changes in their personal life, and so on. As I mention these possibilities, I watch as they confirm, through their body language, the aforementioned positive feelings.

My conclusion? When we ourselves envision the possibility of change, and when we know our desired outcome, our brain does not react so negatively. This information gives us a key clue to our relationship with change: the context around change has a huge impact on our brain.

Here's another concept we've already explored that applies in this situation: the brain's "comfort zone" is connected to this resistance to change. Our brains are convinced that always making sure we know what is coming and what to do next—in other words, staying in our comfort zone—is superior to venturing into the unknown, period. Let's try to understand exactly why our brain has such a positive preference for the comfort zone, along with the ways it tries to keep us there at any cost. After all, the brain is always trying to keep us within this zone, by sending messages that lead us to stay there as long as possible. Whether we are conscious of it or not, we all have an inner voice that incessantly sends comfort zone–promoting signals—"Everything is fine," "Stay with what you know," "This is safe," "This is correct," "It's too risky to try something new," and so on.

Without a doubt, you know someone who is characterized by a "we have always done it this way" attitude. Perhaps you know a lot of people like that! Well, let's be honest with ourselves, and recognize that in certain circumstances *we are* that person. Our fixed mindset whispers this mantra inside our minds frequently. We differ only in how much we are controlled by that voice.

The Discomfort of Comfort

Now let's delve more precisely into what I mean by the comfort zone. There are several different ways to define this concept, but all refer to a mindset or a state of being that keeps us functioning in a calm and controlled way (and so avoids activating our survival mode). We might say the comfort zone is "those situations in life in which we know the rules," or where we feel at ease. In effect, it can also be called "a settled method of working that requires little effort and yields only barely acceptable results."

I personally prefer the first definition, because it's relatively neutral. Feeling safe is certainly not a negative thing, but it doesn't always represent a good situation for us. It's important to clarify that, despite the word "comfort," our comfort zone is not necessarily always a pleasant or positive thing.

It may be, for example, that my work environment is not the healthiest, or perhaps I have a bullying boss. If I am already used to my non-ideal situation, I may fear that it would actually be much more tedious or problematic to look for a new job. Since I am used to my current circumstances, *even if they are not comfortable*, my brain keeps sending me messages that I am in control, in my comfort zone, and so everything's… not necessarily fine, but *known*. And maybe we actually can occasionally control some minor aspects of such scenarios, but any negative situation will affect us negatively at one point or another.

As a coach I have worked with many managers whose attitudes were compatible with a harassing personality—a.k.a. bullies. I have had to become something of an expert on that subject. On the other hand, I've also coached many people who were suffering from a boss who had these characteristics. I've learned a lot from these disparate groups. I've especially learned how to identify the many excuses both bullies and their victims find to avoid generating change.

The insights in this book can help you nurture teams to keep them happier and more successful throughout the change process, but for now, let's return to the reasons we avoid change, as well as how we do so. The mind's ability to create stories to avoid transformation is amazing. I've dealt so extensively with these situations that I've learned to read the real messages hidden between the lines of people's endless excuses. I remember the case of one manager who had not told me that her boss was a bully. She spoke only of her own inability to respond adequately at work and her own lack of productivity. Her mind had convinced her that she was the only one with a problem—that she herself was the sole person who was in the wrong.

It took several sessions to give her a broader perspective on her position, and to help her understand that she was in a dead-end situation. I knew that as long as she kept thinking that everything bad in her work environment stemmed from her actions and attitudes alone, she would not be able to generate any real change. After a lot of thought and discussion, she recognized that her boss's negative personality was having a huge impact. Our job, at that juncture, was to build a strategy to confront her boss and to finally generate positive changes.

You see, when we know the rules, we think we know how to handle what's coming, which gives us a false sense of control. And we believe we have *already* adapted—so we do not want to invest any additional effort to make further changes! We feel that we already know what can and will happen and—although we may not like it—we believe we at least can tolerate it.

Through our comfort zone–favoring neurology, we are in essence internally repeating the old proverb "better the devil you know than the devil you don't"—over and over and over.

But the deeper reason we stay put and avoid change doesn't actually involve our feelings. The brain has a totally different intention when it labors to keep us in the comfort zone as long as possible. It is motivated by the prospect of saving energy!

You see, our brain has a primary, basic goal for our subsistence: to save energy. Remember that while the brain represents about 2 percent of our total body mass, it consumes 20 percent of our total energy. This heavy-energy-consuming organ knows that it must save that energy as much as possible to be prepared for emergencies. And survival is always the highest priority.

The probability of facing such a threat is quite low in our current era, but the reptilian part of our five brains nonetheless takes control whenever it senses *any* external threat. That ancient brain is very well prepared to survive, whether that means attacking, escaping, or staying still (the fight-flight-freeze response).

What Our Brain's Reaction to Change Means for Business

This fundamental brain response has enormous implications in the business context. So, even before we expand our understanding of the mechanisms our five brains use to keep us in the comfort zone, I would like to give an example of what typically happens in companies when they are in the process of implementing changes.

Nowadays, given the ongoing, rapid shifts in tech and business best practices—as well as the impacts of COVID-19—most companies are going through massive changes. They don't have a choice! In general, businesses need to develop and implement an intentional, agile change management plan to ensure those changes go as smoothly as possible.

Change management processes involve two major steps: the preparation of the plan and the implementation phase. The planning in itself rarely involves any problems. There may be minor disagreements or questions about the precise changes desired by various stakeholders, but once company leaders know what they want, the rest of step one mainly involves filling in the blanks of a change management template. There are many excellent templates for building such plans on the market. Some companies even develop their own plans. Most of the big consulting firms offer templates for, and various levels of assistance with, these kinds of plans. Again, this part of the process almost never presents much of a challenge.

The second step is where companies start to face issues. You might assume that once you've determined what change you want and what you need to do to manifest that change, it's merely a matter of making those things happen. But this phase is actually exponentially more complicated—and it's where the highest level of failures and mistakes occur. That is, the significant difficulties in any change management process unfold in the implementation phase. Complications, errors, and full-on failures happen in the process of putting those seemingly perfectly designed plans into practice in real life, with real live human beings—all of whom possess their own pesky brains. Yes, because of the human factor, the implementation process rarely matches with top management expectations.

In short, the process deteriorates because companies are not able to properly manage what is happening in people's brains. Leaders assume that implementation is a rational process. "Our people understand that we need to change," they reason, "and they will thus be able to implement the necessary changes by following the plan, so there shouldn't be any problems."

The problem is that *any* change triggers a chain of reactions in people's emotional and reptilian brains. If those reactions are not taken into consideration, they will become a barrier to the change process at any level. As you can see, the relationship between our brain and the process of change can be problematic.

Now let's analyze the brain mechanisms that prevent us from making changes. One key player in our brain when we are facing changes is the amygdala. This structure, which is made up of nerve tissue, is integrally involved in the brain's fear circuitry. (We say "the" amygdala, but the truth is that we have two, one in each hemisphere.) The amygdala is part of our second brain—the emotional or limbic brain. It has myriad functions, many of which are connected with emotions and behaviors. Here, though, we will look specifically into its fear-processing function.

In a sense, the amygdala acts like an internal traffic light or radar system, sensing—all the time—if anything around us is dangerous. When the amygdala senses a threat, it sends a neural message to our reptilian brain to wake up and activate our fight-flight-freeze defense mechanism. This process takes a fifth of a second, but it initiates two very significant and specific reactions. First, that protective or defense mechanism gets activated, meaning our brain shifts to survival mode. But something else is happening, too, a consequence that most of us are unaware of: our rational brain gets deactivated.

In other words, when we feel fear we cannot think properly. Yet, consider how people typically react to a person who is experiencing an "amygdala hijack"—that is, someone who is controlled by their emotions and instincts. People will commonly tell that "out-of-control" person to "calm down and be rational." Do you think that is an effective approach? If things were that simple, so many of our human conflicts would never have happened!

Six Seconds Is Not Enough

Once the reptilian brain takes control, the way back to rational control is neither fast nor easy. The "six-second rule," which refers to the time it takes the chemicals that are released during an amygdala hijacking to dissipate, suggests one possible remedy. Taking this amount of time to focus on something pleasant will prevent your amygdala from seizing control and causing an emotional reaction while diminishing your thinking capacity. But the main condition for the six-second rule to work is that you need to be in control in the first place in order to remember to follow the rule. This, as you might imagine, doesn't happen very often.

What happens instead? And how does this cycle impact us? We already know that when our amygdala traffic light turns red, our fear circuitry is activated, triggering our reptilian brain response. In a nutshell, we then—almost instantly!—develop tunnel vision. We cannot see the whole forest or the big picture. Furthermore, the parts of our brain where we generate new ideas and resources are shut off. This happens almost constantly in high-pressure corporate environments.

When I present this concept in my workshops, participants often question it, arguing that, in high-pressure situations ("in survival mode"), they actually get *more* creative. It is important to clarify that when we refer to being completely in survival mode, we mean that the reptilian brain is in control. Yes, in this state, we can sometimes access creative ideas, but with only one goal: to survive! All of our energy (and, therefore, ideas) will be oriented toward finding the way out of this pressure cooker. Trust me, this is not the ideal state of mind for innovation and creativity.

On the other hand, we can be genuinely creative under pressure if the prefrontal cortex, or rational brain, is in control. If the reptilian brain is in the lead, the best and truest kind of innovation is not going to happen. Distinguishing between these two states is tricky, especially since many of us feel that we perform better under pressure. Have you ever noticed yourself getting more and more productive and creative as you get closer to a deadline? In such situations, though, the truth is that our rational brain is still in control. A very thin but highly important line separates these two states.

When you train yourself to be productive under pressure, you are in effect training yourself to keep that crucial rational control in place—and to keep your reptilian brain under control. This is what happens with individuals in high-risk professions, such as firefighters, paramedics, emergency room specialists, and so on. They learn how to ensure the slower rational brain stays in control, even when the speedy reptilian brain gets activated.

So, the good news is that the amygdala can be trained. Once the amygdala feels that it's not in a "dangerous" situation (meaning, any perceived "new" situation) and knows itself to be safe and in control, it will neither activate the survival mechanism nor block the rational brain.

Change Is Not Going Away

Those in the professions I listed are not the only ones who are affected by this fear circuitry. Most people in the business world face similar challenges. Nowadays, markets are increasingly competitive and challenging, and the pressure to achieve any and all objectives is on a continual upward slope with no sign of leveling off. And if that was the case over the last few years in the business world, imagine the many ways in which the coronavirus caused an even higher level of intensity.

Clearly, the global pandemic increased the pressure to perform exponentially across the entire corporate sphere. Managers at all levels were (and still are) asking: How can we recover months, possibly years, of lost sales? How can we keep investors interested in our project or our company? How do we convince them that it is time to invest even more… without a strategic plan that ensures return on investment and other ongoing investor benefits? How on earth can we keep our team motivated when they know the odds of downsizing are on the rise? When they are being urged to recover on losses without the additional resources needed to do so?

We could go on and on with distressing examples from daily corporate life in these challenging times. That means we need to prioritize frank conversations about the changes that are already here—and how to best navigate those that are on the horizon. With all the upheavals being thrown at us by a chaotic world, how do we as leaders stay centered and generate proactive, transformative choices, rather than being simply whipped about by the winds of change?

First and foremost, the name of the game these days is survival. But we're not talking about quite the same sort of survival our ancient ancestors needed to pull off. In the current era, only those who manage to keep their amygdala under the control of the rational brain will be able to triumph. This is not a matter of intelligence, nor even of experience. We are co-creating a new reality, and the amygdala has no evolutionary or historical record of a similar context from the past, therefore it must learn. The red-light amygdala learns in an abrupt, chaotic, less productive way, whereas the green-light amygdala has a healthier learning curve in every sense of the word. To survive, and to *thrive*, we must develop the capacity to stay in the green-light zone!

Having dawned rife with some of the biggest challenges humanity has ever encountered, the current decade is ripe for establishing new paradigms around the concept of change. What will the new normal look like? Nobody knows yet, but we do know one thing: under these circumstances, the wise brain cannot continue to deceive itself by pretending that change is not the only constant in life. Likewise, leaders and companies that want to thrive in this ever-changing context must actively accept this reality—and use every tool at their disposal to become more flexible, more adaptive.

Evolving to the next level of adaptability is within our grasp. We are, in effect, training our brain and thereby affecting the amygdala, all the time. The moment we feel we already know what's going on, the amygdala switches to a green-light state. This happens primarily when we are able to recall past experiences that are similar to what we are experiencing right now. That recognition coaches the brain and amygdala to be accustomed to a generally green status.

Don't get me wrong, it's not necessarily an uneventful or extremely repetitive life that keeps the amygdala calm. Rather, our astute understanding and acknowledgment of our daily reality can keep that green light steadily shining. So, consciously developing the capacity to accept that the only constant in life is change, along with the ability to recognize that in many cases we cannot foresee the changes to come, is another way to train the amygdala. Even if our reality entails constant, relentless changes, we can get to a place where the amygdala will remain calm without any problem. We can practice and refine certain skills to ensure this fear-circuitry trigger will not (over)react and our rational brain will stay in control.

Let's revisit the scenario in our brain when we feel fear, adding some further details en route to exploring solutions. We know that our survival mode is activated virtually from the instant we feel under threat. At that point, several other neurological processes unfold. For one, our brain generalizes the feeling of being under threat. What does this mean, exactly? It means that our brain essentially decides that anything and everything is potentially dangerous. Thus, we start to see our environment through a lens of fear—and to deem situations as threatening that would not trigger such feelings of being in danger under green-light circumstances.

This reaction is quite easy to observe in life in general, and in organizations in particular. If we watch closely, we can discern abundant instances in which we and others view relationships with clients, colleagues, or bosses from a fear-based perspective. We can see the pervasiveness of fear when rumors of layoffs or problems in the company begin to circulate freely through the corridors and/or through social media. Imagine all those active amygdalae!

Those most sensitive (reactive) to the feeling of fear will typically then start to come up with more and more stories of how the company is in danger and how the bosses are acting accordingly, and risking the safety of the employees. One quite common negative situation arises when people get to talking about a "blacklist" of those who are going to be fired. Despite a lack of factual evidence, employees at any level may also engage in speculation around an escalating list of threats that in most cases has no basis in reality. The inconvenience of these kinds of reactions is that this "pessimistic mode" lasts longer in our brain and so has enduring repercussions. We find similar situations in social interactions and in the political realm. Certain politicians are quite aware of this human reaction and know how to leverage it in their favor by using our natural fear reaction to rally support for whatever they promise.

Along with the amygdala, another key player in our brain's protective, change-avoidance system is our most primitive brain, the reptilian or lizard brain, which is responsible for controlling our basic functions: sustenance, survival, and sex. Remember that this brain has been part of our existence for more than 500 million years. In spite of its many shortcomings in our modern context, it has an extraordinarily strong influence on our behavior and reactions.

In its energy-saving mission to avoid changes, our brain creates an alliance between the amygdala and the reptilian brain, uniting these two "warriors" to provide immunity to change. This partnership works hard to prevent us from making and, especially, accepting changes.

Our brain's reaction to change can be likened to the "stages of grief" described by Elisabeth Kübler-Ross, the famed Swiss American psychiatrist and hospice pioneer. Kübler-Ross, who worked primarily with terminally ill patients, was one of the

first medical doctors who actively chose to care for such individuals. Before she transformed end-of-life care, any patient
who was dying without hope of treatment was typically
left under the care of nurses, nuns, or hospital volunteers.

Over the years, Kübler-Ross noticed a repetitive pattern
in the ways her patients went through the process of dying.
She defined those stages as shock, denial, anger, bargaining,
depression, and acceptance. Only when the acceptance stage
was reached were her patients truly able to deal with their
situation.

Kübler-Ross's work changed the way we support terminally ill people in countless ways. Moreover, we've learned
that those stages don't only happen when we are dying. We
go through the same stages in any traumatic life situation.

And we also go through similar phases when confronting
change. When a change is unexpected or perceived as negative, or when we don't have the power to make decisions
about (or control the elements of) a change, we react in
ways that echo the stages of Kübler-Ross's model. In change,
as with grief, we cannot escape any of these stages. Our
only potential recourse is to speed up the process—when
possible.

It's important to note that these "stages of change" work
a bit differently in our brain than they do in Kübler-Ross's
description. As our understanding of how the brain works
has grown, we've learned that this process does not occur
in a linear way. For one thing, the stages of change are not
activated one after the other in our emotional brain; on the
contrary, all of these states coexist at the same time. And
rather than utilizing just one area of the brain to manage
information in an orderly, sequential fashion, our resource-
ful brains draw simultaneously from different, interconnected
parts of the brain (including the emotional) to make sense of

any situation in any given moment. Recall, as well, that our emotional brain has a different perception of time. So we can actually move back and forth from one stage to another, and from there to yet another stage, many, many times—even in the same day—until our brain is able to fully embrace the emotional state of acceptance. Only then can we move on.

Here is the linear curve for how we process change (read: knowledge of death) according to the Kübler-Ross model:

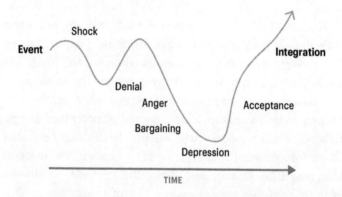

And this is how our brain manages the different stages of the process of change:

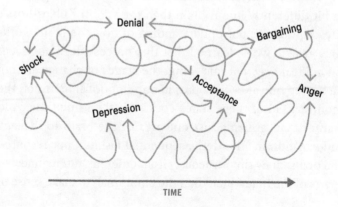

Are you wondering which of these stages is the most common in organizations and business? Denial! In any change process there is a high risk of this emotion. That's why you'll hear:

- "This change is not going to happen."
- "Everything will stay the same."
- "I've been through this before so many times and we always end up back in the same place."
- "I'm not going to risk my neck messing with what's always worked."
- "This CEO will be fired soon and all will be back to the usual."
- "They need to show that something has to change, but it's not going to work."
- "Let's keep doing the same thing as before; this change is temporary and won't stick."

How many times have you heard these or similar sentences? Now that you've come to understand the root causes of these anti-change sentiments, I'll bet you're ready to open yourself up as a pro-transformation leader.

Know Yourself

The truth: there are times when the fear reaction is normal—and even necessary. In those moments when I feel I am genuinely in danger, I must consider the worst possible scenarios in order to be prepared to protect and defend myself. But our fear circuitry's valiant efforts can also be debilitating, especially when they are triggered too often by things that don't pose a threat to our survival at all—thereby causing us to lose our most valuable neural tools when we may need them most. Thus, we often pay a price in the contemporary world for the strategies our brain developed to protect us millennia ago. The more we know about ourselves, and the more we train our amygdala to stay in the green zone, the less we will be hindered by these now-useless reactions. The practices and information you have read so far in this chapter will help you circumvent your outdated fear circuitry and thus stay present, fully functional, and truly creative in the face of everyday change.

Self-awareness and self-understanding, along with the ensuing ability to retain self-control, are arguably the most imperative characteristics of effective leadership. Who is in control of *your* brain? As a conscious, self-aware leader, you must have the capacity to observe your own fear reaction and know what to do about it. You should be able to notice when an external situation (in this case, change) is triggering an internal reaction that's activating your reptilian brain and plunging your amygdala into the red—and you must deploy strategies that keep your rational brain in control. The strategies at the end of this chapter will enable you to do just that.

In the next chapter, we'll discuss change on the organizational level, paying close attention to what happens in our brains when the amygdala is calm, or in the green-light mode, and our rational brain is in control. When the amygdala isn't busy registering a threatening situation around us (and remember, we can train it to see change as safe!), our vast warehouse of brainy resources remains open. We can access all of the parts of our brains where we can find extensive information and get new ideas—and we can put those ideas into action. Our perspective shifts from tunnel vision to wide angle, and our perception of what is happening is closer to reality. In addition, we can mobilize the positive emotions that will help us move forward and get things done.

In other words, staying in the green zone enables us to gladly and effectively think about, initiate, and execute change. This healthy, upbeat attitude toward change is exactly what you want for yourself and your team, right? In Chapter 5, you'll learn how to achieve that goal.

PRACTICES TO SOOTHE YOUR FEAR CIRCUITRY

Before we get into organization-level changes, you'll want to begin to explore and train your own fear circuitry. Here are two exercises to get you started.

EXERCISE 1: The Six-Second Fear Buster

It's literally possible to change your neurology in under ten seconds! Sounds too good to be true? The catch is this: since we're hardwired to focus more on the negative, you'll need to practice this exercise consistently to see real benefits over time.

STEP 1: First, let's create a positive vision. Think about a good experience or hoped-for outcome at work. For example, you might envision your team producing the best possible results in a current project, or imagine yourself achieving success in a critical performance area. Try to bring in as many senses as possible. If you prefer a fully sensory approach, look around you for something uplifting to focus on (perhaps an award or other tangible evidence of accomplishment and growth), listen with full attention to a beautiful piece of music, or use another pleasurable experience as your primary focus.

STEP 2: Explore this happy thought, vision, sound, taste, or whatever it is for at least six seconds. Be sure to keep your entire attention on this positive thing, so you can train your brain to search for and strengthen neural pathways that lead toward positive growth and happiness—and away from fear and other negative triggers.

STEP 3: Repeat often!

When we create and reinforce those positive pathways, positive behavior follows. As six-second breaks become a habit, you'll be ready to apply this strategy under more challenging circumstances. Try this six-second fear buster the next time you feel yourself begin to react negatively to a new situation, or whenever a little bit of goodness might be helpful!

VARIATION FOR TRIGGERED SITUATIONS: When our reptilian brain is activated, it's not easy to access optimistic, encouraging thoughts. This exercise can be adapted to bring a positive approach to a negative (red-light) situation. When you find yourself in seemingly trapped in survival mode, try a more practical phrase or mantra: "I can deal with this," "I'm going to find a tool to overcome this obstacle," and so on. Repeat it slowly aloud, once with your eyes closed, once with your eyes open. That should get you to six seconds! Repeat as often as possible until your rational brain gains ascendancy.

EXERCISE 2: Grown-Up Red Light/Green Light

Keeping your amygdala in the green zone is key. As you learned in this chapter, you can train your amygdala to react differently when you consistently frame change and difference as safe and commonplace. Here's one effective way to be your own amygdala coach.

STEP 1: Think of something you do in the same way every day. It should be something that could be done differently. For example, let's say you spend the first hour of each day reaching out to clients via phone while seated at your desk and facing your computer.

STEP 2: Think of as many potential changes you can make to this routine as possible (for example, switching the time, communication medium, view, seat, and so on) and then consider the various ways in which you might implement those changes. The importance of this is that we are trying to avoid traveling the same pathways in the brain—the ones that keep our amygdala in the red zone. Making small changes is like taking a different route. That new landscape will trigger different thoughts, and, therefore, different behaviors.

STEP 3: As you repeat this process, varying each element, breathe deeply and remind yourself at each juncture that change is safe, positive, helpful. You might say to yourself, "Doing things differently helps my brain stay agile," or "Transformation is an ordinary and important part of life, and helps us grow into our best selves," or perhaps even, "Experimenting with changes is a safe, common, necessary part of innovation."

STEP 4: If you feel yourself reacting to even these minor changes, redouble your efforts to self-soothe with slow, full breaths and calming words. It may be helpful to make your exhalations longer than your inhalations, as this soothes the body's fear circuitry as well. Continue to reframe changes as safe and normal. Some of the stress management exercises from Chapter 3, such as the Rule of Five, can also be implemented here.

Consider extending this exercise to higher-risk changes, maintaining these approaches to keep your amygdala in green-light status.

5

Brain-Smart
Organizational Change

OW THAT I've described the whole spectrum of change-resistant components in our brains, and we've accepted the fact that change is—now, more than ever—omnipresent, let's see how to embrace and enhance the change process in the business sphere. With the right approach, you can leverage your leadership position to effectively and fearlessly lead your team through any change process, including major, company-wide transformation.

That may seem daunting, given the usual human-hindered outcomes of most attempted corporate changes. Don't panic! Our brains are perfectly prepared to overcome their natural barriers to change—but only with the right tools. That's where you, the brain-smart leader, come in.

In my opinion, the clearest way to understand how to achieve real, lasting change involves conceptualizing our "selves" as made up of biological hardware and software. We can call our brain our hardware. It houses the necessary systems for our proper functioning. Within this hardware, I want to highlight a particular brain function that has become a very popular topic over the last few years. As is often the case with "new" concepts, the original discovery was made many years ago and has only just recently reached the mainstream. I am referring to the concept of neuroplasticity.

Although it wasn't widely used until the 1960s, the term "neuroplasticity" was first used in 1948 by the Polish neuroscientist Jerzy Konorski to describe observed changes in neuronal structure. Neuroplasticity, also known as brain plasticity or neural plasticity, is the ability of the brain to undergo biological changes, ranging from the cellular level (individual neurons) all the way to large-scale changes involving cortical remapping. In short, the brain has the potential to change and grow over time in response to its environment. Maybe the old saying "you can't teach an old dog new tricks" isn't true after all!

There are two types of neuroplasticity. Functional plasticity is the brain's amazing ability to move functions from a damaged area of the brain to other undamaged areas. Structural plasticity is the brain's likewise remarkable capacity to actually change its physical structure as a result of learning. Here, I need to be fair to Santiago Ramón y Cajal, who won the Nobel Prize in Physiology or Medicine (jointly with Camillo Golgi) in 1906. Decades before Konorski, Ramón y Cajal, a Spanish neuroanatomist said, "Any man could, if he were so inclined, be the sculptor of his own brain." And we must assume that some wise thinkers have suspected for centuries, if not millennia, that the brain is a dynamic, potentially *changeable* aspect of our being.

Nonetheless, the concept of neuroplasticity tore apart a very old paradigm that had prevailed in medicine for many, many years. In that model, the human brain was thought to experience peak neural development only up until adolescence; from there, it was essentially a downhill process. No doubt this concept was highly depressing!

Luckily, more recent findings on neuroplasticity have clearly demonstrated otherwise. Our brain actually produces new neurons throughout our entire lifetime. That means it is able to rewire itself any time, and at any age.

In my workshops, I like to present this concept in a provocative way by telling my audience that there is literally no excuse for not changing. How many times have you heard people justifying their behavior or fear of change by saying, "This is just the way I am"? Sound familiar? Any time you hear someone repeat this sort of sentiment, feel free to say, "You are the way you are because you choose to be that way." Obviously, you may want to find more tactful language, but bear in mind at all times the truth behind it. Each and every one of us has the power to make changes in our brain.

This leads us to the second key player involved in the process of generating changes: our software, that is, our mind. The famous twentieth-century Austrian neurologist and psychiatrist Viktor Frankl, who spent three years in a Nazi concentration camp—probably the worst conceivable social and human injustice a civilian could suffer—had much to say on this subject. When he was captured, he had been working for some time as a psychiatrist in the city of Vienna. Frankl's wife and in-laws died in the concentration camps—he was the only person from his family to survive the war, and he lived on afterward for many years and wrote many books. In his most famous book, *Man's Search for Meaning*, he delved into the concentration camp experience.

I have always found his words about how to live life to be among the most powerful and compelling ever written. He said, "Everything can be taken from a man but one thing:

the last of human freedoms—to choose one's attitude in any given set of circumstances."

We always, absolutely always, retain the right to decide how to react to any external situation. This truth encompasses every single event and interaction in our lives (including how we talk to ourselves!), but it's not necessarily easy to accept or embrace.

So, we can have different attitudes, and it's up to us to manage those attitudes, much like we manage others to the best of our ability and in hopes of the best outcome. Here's something fascinating, though: we now know that different attitudes have different pathways in the brain, and therefore produce different outcomes in our brains *as well as in real life!* This indicates that attitude is a crucial component of our software that also impacts our hardware, our brains. Science has yet to decide whether what we call the *mind* is a product of the brain, but in my view the brain is the *executor* of the mind's decisions and attitudes. So, the impact of what goes on in our minds, all the way down to the infinitesimal scale of our neurons, is pervasive, vitally shaping our mental landscape and how we experience life.

I've mentioned that we produce new neurons during our whole lives. To keep things simple, let's call these new neurons "baby neurons." The power of our neurons lies in their ability to make connections with other neurons. We also know today that every neuron in our brain is connected to at least 10,000 other neurons. Neurons are team players! When a neuron is unable to make connections, it is barely able to survive. Baby neurons can stay in our neural systems only so long as they are able to make connections. To have enough strength to do so, they need food. And I'm not talking only about glucose. The three main types of "food" that allow neurons to make connections are learning, having new experiences, and physical activity. In other words, in order to survive, they (and, therefore, we!) need to be ingesting information or going through novel experiences, including varied physical activity.

A negative attitude—defined here as any stance that is characterized by refusing or resisting new changes, ideas, or information—does not provide food for these baby neurons. Thus, negative attitudes basically kill baby neurons through starvation. It sounds a bit dramatic, doesn't it? Yet, it's certainly true. So, while shocking my clients or audience with this fact is part of my goal, my other aim is to wake them up to the vast possibilities offered by a more positive attitude.

This surprising information is also enormously useful for leaders hoping to inspire their teams. When we extrapolate the previous chapter's fear circuitry–soothing techniques to a group/business context and add in the impact of realizing that the brain's inherent resistance to change causes us to starve our own wee baby neurons, we have a potent recipe for driving transformation. Yet we must also bear in mind that, when it comes to people's egos and livelihoods, staying in the steady status quo, in the realm where you "already know everything," can feel all the more imperative to personal survival. And yet attitudes like these—thinking we know everything, or that things will ever stay the same—are entirely based on the illusion that stasis is possible. Things change all the time, no matter what!

Furthermore, those individuals who are always supplying pushback on any new project, or refusing to confront challenges, or saying "We can't do this!" are not feeding their neurons. Change-resistant people are not giving their neurons learning opportunities, or any reason to connect with other neurons. In other words, their baby neurons have a high probability of not surviving. By killing off our potential-packed young brain cells, a negative attitude literally takes us to a dead end. And in the meantime, when we attempt to perpetuate the status quo, we strengthen the same old pathways in the brain, thereby reinforcing the habits and behaviors that haven't served us well.

And here's another big problem negative attitudes bring to the table: in general, they are highly contagious.

Look closely at those teams wherein some of the members choose a negative attitude to express or inhabit their position. In one way or another, those team members will generate doubts and misgivings for the rest of the team. This happens because the reptilian brain's survival mode is our most immediate, natural response to any real or potential negativity. We have to actively "fight" this response in ourselves if we want to master our brains—and so does everyone else on the team who wants to participate proactively. Otherwise, even just one naysayer can very quickly contaminate the whole team.

On the other hand, a positive attitude is also contagious! In this context, I define being positive as having the willingness to actively face changes and challenges. Believe it or not, this type of attitude is not necessarily linked with a given individual's personality style or the way they express themselves on a daily basis. As we saw in the eighth tool in Chapter 3, an employee with a positive attitude toward change could have a grumpy, even unpleasant personality under most circumstances, but any time the team is facing problems, they will be the first to say, "Let me try," or "I will do it."

This reaction implies a leap of faith. Stating "I will try" means that I believe I can somehow—perhaps with great effort—find a solution. And that I am ready and willing to make that effort. This is the real meaning of being positive.

Remember (again, from Chapter 3) that a positive attitude is not necessarily connected to being happy. It's about the ways in which someone is disposed to bring ideas into action, even in the face of difficulties—and it's about the concrete outcomes that flow from that attitude. It's so good to know that while we cannot be happy all of the time, we can be positive most or all of the time!

A New Change Equation

These days, when a company decides to introduce changes, it starts by preparing a change plan that carefully considers and outlines all the many, many necessary steps and details for their implementation. And then... the real difficulties begin.

It's at this stage that any company faces its greatest threat to transformation—the strongest barrier that undermines any real possibility that this change plan will be successfully executed: people's brains.

Having discussed in the previous chapter the change-resistant mechanisms of the mind, along with techniques for overcoming these barriers, we can recognize that an extremely specific plan is required for any fruitful enterprise change process. Now, I am about to present a six-step implementation plan that will exponentially increase the chances of an effective execution.

What we must first understand, though, is the objective of this plan. In other words, we need to clearly comprehend what we are aiming for if our efforts to increase our chances of success are to bear fruit. Our goal is to train the amygdala and calm down the reptilian brain. Just as dealing with our fear circuitry is critical when we want to achieve personal growth, we will only be able to incorporate changes on the corporate level when these ancient neural habits are effectively addressed.

This chapter's tool entails a series of six steps, which I will explore at length throughout the following pages. These steps represent the essential elements of brain-smart corporate change. Taken together, they offer a road map to genuine transformation for your team and your enterprise—at any scale.

SIX STEPS TO BRAIN-SMART CORPORATE CHANGE

1 Create a compelling vision.
2 Make change familiar.
3 Get people involved.
4 Take small steps toward big changes.
5 Leverage company connectors.
6 Apply the Attention Density Formula.

Even though this list conveys the right order for correct implementation, I will begin my explanation with the second step. Why? Because the first step is the most important, so I prefer to expand on it at length after I've described the five that follow it.

These steps apply to organizations that decide to implement a change in their structures or systems. They detail the strictly delineated process of implementation necessary to generate acceptance and commitment from employees.

Let's begin our road map.

Step 2—Make Change Familiar

We have discussed at length how the brain reacts in the face of the unknown. Remember that the brain needs information to build those potential scenarios it's always working on. As it turns out, the less information it receives, the more it will build "imaginary" futures—and not necessarily the most positive ones. After all, it has to prepare the system for the worst, just in case. On a biological level, the amygdala has to be in constant red-light alert mode if there is any threat around. Thus, so long as there's a possibility that we could be in danger in any way, the amygdala stays in control, vigilant and ready.

Don't get me wrong, this is the way it should be when we need to protect ourselves and stay safe. All of this robust and interrelated fear circuitry evolved based on information from experiences in the distant past that caused humans to develop this highly responsive, precise, comprehensive neural system and so allowed us to survive. In those days, the faster any information from our environment was processed, the better. That speed gave us more time for this circuitry to react and then, ideally, allowed us the leeway to then rationally decide the best course of action, thereby avoiding reacting without thinking.

Returning to our current context, let's say top management decides to introduce changes in the organization. Handled incorrectly (and that refers to nearly every instance), even the slightest hint of those changes will almost inevitably provoke feelings of uncertainty and fear throughout the company.

In general, the information that changes are coming almost always seeps into the organization prior to its intended arrival—and that's when the gossip begins. How can leadership prevent the worst of the gossip? By giving employees' brains enough time to digest the situation. And how to do that? By confirming that changes are underway and providing as much information to as many people as possible, as early as possible.

When I work with managers in companies that are facing this situation, they often share with me that the process of arriving to an adequate plan takes not only time, but also many steps—some forward, some sideways... some even backward. What is the point, most managers wonder, of informing everybody about something that most likely is not in its final version? Won't that just create more fear and confusion in the interim? And, yes, this approach is correct and fair, but we have to be brain-smart, too. So, I recommend informing employees from the outset that the final plan has not yet been hammered out, and explaining that this incomplete status is the reason why no details are being reported. How is this vague news helpful? It's quite simple: telling people that a plan is being formulated (but is not yet firmly defined) gives them much-needed information, however incomplete.

A related example from my coaching and consultancy work provides a good illustration of these phenomena. A few years ago, I was working with a group of leaders from a European manufacturing company. We had been meeting periodically for months as part of a leadership development process. We knew each other well and seemed to have no problems sharing information.

One day, I was not able to find a way to motivate them or keep their focus and attention on our work together. I decided to stop the formal training and asked them directly what was happening. They informed me that there were rumors that a production plant was going to be closed. If so, chances were that about four hundred people were going to be laid off. The rest of the day became a group coaching session, in which we strove to figure out how the participants should deal with such a daunting possibility.

The next day, I called my contact in HR and asked her what was happening. She confirmed that there was an issue, but when I asked her if she knew what the final decision was going to be, she said she did not. Apparently, that decision was going to be made in the company's U.S. headquarters and the European branches had not yet been informed.

Once I heard this, my recommendation as a coach was for the company to organize a meeting with the entire plant and tell them exactly that: yes, the rumors are true, but the local senior management lacks more information. This intervention had an almost magical effect! Both employees and managers were able to calm down. Everyone at the plant waited, together with the top managers, for that final decision. In the end, the plant was not closed, but—because of the leadership's open approach—the individuals on that team would have been in a stronger position moving forward whatever the outcome.

Saying that there is no concrete information is a form of information. Even this inherently limited level of openness can produce a marked increase in confidence and trust in leadership, in part because—as in the case I just described—it shows that all involved are on the same side.

So, confirm those rumors, if they're true, and give employees' brains enough time to process the information in order to eventually reach the acceptance stage. Let them talk all they want about change. They'll be sharing their feelings about change, getting accustomed to the normalcy of impending changes, and even learning from each other about how to deal with those changes.

To help you reach that point, here are a few tips for making change familiar:

- Support "watercooler conversations" about change. These days, this may mean "virtual happy hours" or informal conference calls to share casual dialogue around business happenings.

- Share stories of successful change from your company or a similar one.

- Bring a speaker in to talk about change.

- If your company has a mentoring program, invite your mentors to discuss change with their mentees.

- If your company has a team of internal coaches, have them facilitate group coaching sessions on change—or hire an experienced coach from outside to do the same.

- Encourage your people to vent concerning how they feel about the changes.

If you follow some or all of these recommendations, your people's entire, five-part brains will be prepared for the change to come. As we have seen, familiarity with change and acceptance of its inevitability prepare the amygdala to stay in its more creative, more effective, more successful green zone.

Step 3—Get People Involved

How do you feel when someone tells you to execute a plan by following predetermined guidelines... without giving you any chance to express your opinion or ideas? I'm guessing you don't find it all that motivating or enjoyable. Well, guess what? Your employees don't either.

At the same time, engaging everybody concerned at every stage of change would likely make for a big, slow-moving mess. Fortunately, there is a middle way. There's no question that any corporate-scale change plan must be formulated down to the smallest detail to avoid mistakes and facilitate correct implementation. But this step—involving employees in the process—must be followed assiduously if you want to increase the chances of a successful change implementation. My commitment increases if I am part of the solution. Doesn't yours?

The fundamental framework of any plan should only be defined by the senior managers in the organization. Leadership should bear full responsibility for deciding, broadly, what changes should be incorporated into the organization, as well as when they should occur.

But when it comes to actually implementing them, you should always create room for your employees to make decisions around the details of how those changes will be initiated and executed. I do not mean that you must make changes in the essence of the plan, rather that certain aspects of implementation should be chosen, driven, shaped by the employees.

This will give employees a stake in the process via what's known in the business world as the "IKEA effect." This might sound silly, but one of the reasons people love (and hate) to buy furniture at IKEA is that you must assemble it yourself. This creates an emotional connection with the product: every time you see it, thoughts like "I put that together" or "I was involved in the process" come to your mind, right?

But there's also a brain-based aim for this step. The goal is to create a healthy alliance between the rational brain and the emotional brain. All of our brains must be in alignment to function properly. The emotional impact of change is mitigated if we work with our rational brain on how to implement it. This aligns our rational and emotional brains to better navigate the challenges and details of transformation.

Most of the time, corporations make the same mistake: imposing a step-by-step implementation plan on their biologically change-averse employees. This approach must be avoided for all of the reasons we have been discussing.

Leadership must seek a delicate balance between their perfectly detailed plan and the flexible elements that can be decided—and completed—by the employees themselves. Otherwise, an overly strict, regimented process could lead to stalled, flawed, and/or failed implementation.

When I recommend this step to leaders who are responsible for change, their comments usually follow the same lines: "Yes, I agree, but we cannot involve the whole company in the preparation of the change plan. It will result in total chaos and a never-ending process." And they are right. Let's bear in mind that I'm only referring to those parts of the implementation that can be effectively, safely delegated. That limited but profoundly generative flexibility will make all the difference in your team's perspective on change—and will result in superior outcomes.

Step 4—Take Small Steps toward Big Changes

Sometimes senior managers don't take enough care in the way they inform the rest of the company's workforce about the changes to come. Perhaps another way to put this is that leaders do not understand the magnitude of the effect of certain words on their employees' minds. Announcements are geared toward greatest organizational impact, rather than brain-smart change management. "Big changes ahead!" is the top-down proclamation. Such messages make an extremely negative impression on the brain. In and of themselves, the words "big" and "change" together immediately trigger our fear circuitry. Right away, our amygdala zooms into red-light status. And it's not just the amygdala—our entire brain basically catches on fire!

Let's not even overload our own brains with this notion. Just the concept alone can make our brain fearful. Whether reading this or hearing the "big change" news from top management, that vigilant change-immunity system will typically be shaking things up, instantly and desperately trying to stop any potential situation that might involve the brain in a "big change" process.

We need to feed ourselves and others the process of change through small bites, using the classic Kaizen (a Sino-Japanese-rooted business term for mindful, continuous improvement to achieve greater efficiency and quality) approach: ongoing, small, incremental steps toward the goal.

When big changes are definitely on the horizon, the responsible parties must inform people in the organization from the beginning, presenting the steps of the plan and other relevant information in small, digestible amounts. Timing is another important parameter in this equation, especially as far as an end date goes. A realistic timeline that employees can mentally integrate and, at least on some level, plan for themselves is absolutely required. And if (initially) any or all of this information is not yet available, leadership should be open about that, too.

To be sure, there are instances wherein leaders don't know how deep the change is going to be or when it is going to end. It is nonetheless important for our reactive brain facing changes to understand that there is an ongoing process that is—and will be—unfolding. It helps the brains of all concerned to know that change is happening, even if they don't have all the details and even when those responsible don't know when it's going to be over. Even this limited information is far, far superior to silence.

Whether top management has a multifaceted, complete, firm plan with a solid end date or only a rather vague idea of likely changes, introducing basic information and initiating incremental steps will prepare employees' brains for shifts large or small.

Step 5—Leverage Company Connectors

One key way to ensure that the plan is distributed throughout the organization and to increase the overall chances of acceptance is to work through so-called connectors. Connectors are those employees who are liked and accepted by the majority of people in the organization. They usually know what's happening at all levels of the company, and, if they don't, they know how to find out. They are the ones who easily talk with all of their fellow workers, no matter their position in the hierarchy. Connectors generate followers with ease and grace.

These special individuals become communication hubs, relating to many others in a highly productive fashion. They are equivalent to neurons that have made many more connections than the majority—exceptionally healthy as individuals and extremely vital to the whole. Any important information in the company necessarily goes through them in one way or another. Connectors are easy to identify, and they represent the best ambassadors for everything you want to introduce into the system.

By the way, connectors are not necessarily in high positions in the organization. In most cases, they are at the middle management level or part of an egalitarian team, and not formally in charge. They are, in essence, leaders without a title.

Encourage these remarkable connectors to be involved in the whole process, from design and preparation to execution, and you'll find that overall engagement will increase dramatically. Your work is simply to identify them—they will do the rest.

Step 6—Apply the Attention Density Formula

This concept, first formulated by neuroplasticity expert Jeffrey M. Schwartz in 2006, refers to a method by which it's possible to increase the probability that a change will be permanent.

Schwartz developed the following formula for this method:

Attention Density = exposure to new thoughts, experiences, and suggestions + repetition (reinforcing the learning) + application (providing evidence of consolidation and integration) × more repetition (of the whole process)

In short:

Attention Density = (exposure + repetition + application) × 3

These three elements, reinforced via repetition, will increase the chances of lasting, sustainable change. Without them, any change achieved will probably be tenuous and temporary. Therefore, leadership must ensure that any change plan encompasses the needed energy and time to fully implement the Attention Density Formula.

Acceptance, learning, developing a personal connection/investment—none of these important processes happens in a day. In effect, the brain needs to be bombarded many times to accept, understand, and incorporate any kind of change. At the same time, it comes to understand only through experience. Again, I don't mean a single encounter; the brain understands best through multiple similar experiences.

The brain learns in several related ways: by repetition, trial and error, and by imitating others' behavior through mirror neurons. Our mirror neuron system, located in our prefrontal cortex, allows us to imitate others when their behavior has a purpose. Mirror neurons "fire" both when we are doing something and when we are observing that same action, giving management still more ways—think group activities, online or in-person practice sessions, workshops, videos, and so on—to help employees integrate the various aspects of change. The Attention Density Formula builds up all such healthy neural connections so that the brains of everyone involved are in the green zone: calm, and therefore highly productive, innovative, and engaged.

While top management may aspire to achieve a rigid set of changes in a very specific timeframe, they must be mentally agile enough to understand that the process may take longer than planned if it is to be truly effective and lasting. Familiarizing talent with change, getting them personally involved, taking incremental steps, leaning on connectors as company hubs, and deploying the Attention Density Formula will help ensure the best outcome. But how to hold all these steps together? That's where we come to the first step—the unifying, inspirational element that infuses every other step with its raison d'être.

Step 1—Create a Compelling Vision

Creating a compelling vision is the most important step of my brain-smart change formula, so it needs to be explained properly. A strong, inspiring vision can be an immensely powerful tool to lead companies through the process of transformation.

Creating this vision—your step #1—actually involves two phases. First, leadership is tasked with developing clear concepts and materials that reflect the organization's ultimate purpose, as well as the final scenario to be achieved. Next, leadership needs to share that vision with employees in such a way as to inspire and motivate them. The best medium for this message is usually visual: a graphic or set of graphics presenting the company's aims in a very clear and straightforward—yet also attractive and desirable—fashion.

When the vision representing the final goal is compelling, it will induce a feeling of "I want to be there," thereby adding meaning to the journey—which will in turn inspire people to overcome any barriers or difficulties that arise along the way. As Friedrich Nietzsche said, "Those who have a 'why' to live can bear with almost any 'how.'"

Let's explore this idea of graphic inspiration in the context of how visual input is linked with behaviors. Most people don't realize the incredible impact images have on our behavior. In my workshops, I explain this concept by presenting three different scenarios.

In the first scenario, consider a brick placed at each end of a room. A long, thick, wide wooden board between the two bricks forms a bridge spanning across the room. The whole structure is about four inches high. After describing this scenario to my participants, I ask if they would have any problem walking on the plank from one end of the room to the other. The usual response is a unilateral "no."

In the second scenario, I propose a similarly solid, wide wooden board that spans two buildings that are 65 feet apart and 140 feet high. Now, the image is not the same—and neither is my audience's response. Generally, no one says they'd walk across the void between the two buildings.

In my third scenario, that same thick wooden bridge still reaches between the same two buildings but, now, your infant child is crawling in your direction... across the plank! When I present this image, virtually no one hesitates to say that they would at least try to cross to save the baby.

What am I trying to show with these scenarios? Well, there is no doubt that each image generates different feelings and behaviors, if only hypothetically. In real-life situations, visual input is even more likely to lead to action.

This is what happens to us on a daily basis. We act based on what we see inside our minds. And when we fully comprehend the fact that those images lead to behaviors, we can't help but come to the conclusion that we can only change a behavior if we first change the image of what we want. In other words, if we want real change, we need to change the way we think about—how we *envision*—our situation.

For example, if we want to get healthier, we can impel ourselves toward healthier behaviors by envisioning our healthy, vital, optimal self. But we can't make those changes in our behavior if we are still thinking in the same old way.

When we don't like our own behavior, it's wise to ask to ourselves what image, idea, or belief we may have in our mind that supports that behavior. The same applies to any organization, especially when we look at behaviors (at all levels) when management is trying to introduce a change. It's easy to predict whether that change is going to be successful and sustainable—simply check the way those involved see the company's future. What kind of image is leading that transformation?

There is a famous saying (often, if possibly incorrectly, attributed to Albert Einstein) that insanity is doing the same thing over and over again and expecting different results. When companies try to change multiple times and repeatedly fail, it is because they are skipping the first step of brain-smart change. Pretty insane, right? Also: costly and time-consuming.

So I recommend that, as a leader, you ask yourself a few key questions right from the outset:

- What is my vision for my company?
- What is my vision for my clients?
- What is my vision for my work?

And even:

- What is my vision for myself?

What you come up with can be used to shape your unique and creative perspective on potential corporate change. In the initial phase of this step, senior managers should not be afraid to share together their creative, even daring images, dreams, and ideas for the company's future in order to formulate a change message that will truly inform and inspire employees. After all, the power of a compelling vision is that it leads us through changes without fear, pushing us out of our stale comfort zones and into new adventures in innovation, interconnection, efficiency, and productivity.

As Mahatma Gandhi advised, "If we could change ourselves, the tendencies in the world would also change." In other words, as his wisdom is most often expressed today: "Be the change you want to see in the world."

Remember, vision is what motivates behavior and opens the door for change, not the other way around.

Our brains follow the same patterns in the business world as they do in our personal lives. One example of relevance to both spheres is the perennial conflict that arises when we know we are supposed to change but are not ready to give up certain habits, people, or ways of doing business. The truth is, we often don't really want to change.

The Gatopardismo Effect

Issues around change can also emerge from another human factor: interpersonal dynamics. Often, the need to introduce changes in an organization becomes a tool for exerting top-down, bottom-up, and/or lateral social pressure. I've been in coaching situations in which the leader tells me that everyone in the organization is asking for changes, but that leader can't understand this need because the company is moving in the right direction. Sometimes, such discrepancies reveal a legitimate disconnect between perspectives; in other cases, this kind of social pressure causes more damage than benefits.

Given the current business climate—one in which change is seen as invariably good and necessary—managers may sometimes feel intense pressure to constantly perform in this area. They may be forced to make changes even if they are not convinced those changes are necessary or right for the company—and they therefore may not know exactly what to do to make things work. In many such cases, managers end up applying the "gatopardismo" technique. This concept comes from Giuseppe Tomasi di Lampedusa's 1958 novel *Il Gattopardo* (*The Leopard*), and it basically involves "changing everything so that nothing changes." Widely used in politics, by the way.

Gatopardismo can unfold through conscious or unconscious efforts. It can also be driven by top management and/or caused by employee resistance when changes are not introduced in an effective way—for example, by skipping the steps I have described in this chapter.

So bear in mind that, if you want to introduce changes in a successful way, the very first step is to generate a compelling vision, one that allows those at all levels of the organization to clearly understand the key objectives around those changes. This vision should be based on a meaningful conceptualization of the future that addresses corporate needs and goals, rather than merely changing for the sake of change. It will not necessarily be attractive or beneficial for all employees, but it must encompass the greater good overall.

And let's be honest: while a transformation may impact positively on the organization as a whole, it may not be positive for all employees. Nonetheless, a clear vision is always useful for everyone, even for those who could be negatively impacted. Transparency around future aims allows every individual to decide what they want to do and plan their future accordingly. It also gives employees the capacity to make informed decisions about whether or not to stay in the organization. Remember, any kind of information is better than no information.

Brain-Smart Corporate Change in Action

So let's put our formula in order. Once the vision—step #1— has been created (with the maximum number of details), and shared (in a compelling, ideally visual mode), it is necessary to widely, openly acknowledge that changes are coming— your step #2. When leaders inform employees about change from the outset, the latter can start working with the impending reality; in other words, they can become increasingly and calmly conscious of the fact that those changes are on the way. The target of this step is, as discussed, their amygdalae: the earlier they can start working on the concept, the sooner it's possible to stop their natural cycle of negative reactions when facing uncertainty. Thus, you must carefully plan how to introduce information around the planned changes. At this stage and every other, be sure to incorporate elements of your overall creative, compelling vision of the future.

Then—step #3—think about how each employee will be involved in the implementation process, because they need to be allowed to make decisions if you want them to care about and be invested in the proposed changes. And remember: the more tiny, incremental steps, the better, once the whole team is on board—step #4. We must not overload the brain with big changes that are very difficult to digest all at once. Small steps truly do lead to big changes. Next—step #5— identify the hubs, those super-connected employees who can help with proper implementation. And finally, there's step #6: consistently and regularly lean on the Attention Density Formula for lasting change. The human brain learns by repetition, and this process takes time.

By following these six steps, leaders can increase the probability of successfully initiating and executing sustainable change. Remember that organizational change is imperative in today's world. With the pace of change increasing continuously, it can feel as if management must develop a plan and implement responsive changes immediately at just about every juncture. Neuroscience shows us that the contrary is true.

Leadership must learn to take a step back and find wisdom in both past experience (in our own corporations, as well as what we know from other companies) and in the latest scientific findings. And that's where the Six Steps to Brain-Smart Corporate Change comes into play. Leaders who are able to muster the required patience, insight, and flexibility will find that their change processes involve little or no fear, gossip, and chaos, while producing unprecedented engagement and exceptional success over both the short and long terms.

CREATING YOUR PRELIMINARY OUTLINE

Try incorporating the fear-buster and red-light/green-light practices from Chapter 4 while you sketch out the steps from this chapter as they might be enacted for your particular change projects in your unique organization. This low-stakes, eminently safe drafting exercise will get you accustomed (desensitized) to upcoming change, and prepare you to help your team tackle change in the best way possible. While you won't necessarily share this preliminary plan with your team, it will get your five brains on board and start your creative juices flowing. So, let's dive in!

STEP 1: Find a brainstorming medium that works for you—whether that's a bullet journal, word-processing file, online tool, sketchpad, or something else.

STEP 2: Identify a key change (small or large) that your organization needs to implement.

STEP 3: Go through the six steps described in this chapter one by one as they pertain to this change, jotting down any ideas that come to mind. It's fine to include both fears and hopes along with practical aspects. To that end, welcome input from your gut and heart brains, as well as from your rational and creative ones.

STEP 4: Reflect on your process. How do each of your brains seem to react to these potential changes? How can you use the skills and knowledge you've gained from this and the previous chapter to tackle any reactive tendencies? Finally, what does this exercise reveal to you about helping your team thrive through transformation?

6

Impactful Mindset: The Power of the Right Attitude

W E STARTED our journey here by exploring our multiple brains. We learned how to switch ourselves from a state of constant overwhelm to one featuring healthy habits that take advantage of our five brains' natural propensities and cycles to boost overall performance and satisfaction. We considered ways to encourage similar shifts toward flourishing in the workplace. And, in the previous two chapters, we looked at ways to build neural resilience and agility so that we—and our teams—can handle external changes proactively. Now it's time to look into optimizing some fundamental aspects of how we think by making changes in our attitudes and assumptions that will generate major impact.

Our mindset influences us on every level of existence. It shapes our thoughts, it drives our communications, and, ultimately, it results in the actions we take. But what can we actually *do* with the advantages we've gained via all the insights and practices contained in this book so far? Our mindset determines the answer! So, it's vitally important to approach and manage this foundational aspect of our being wisely. Our wondrous neurology can be harnessed to produce exceptional outcomes far beyond even what we can imagine... if we strive to understand, implement, and consistently nurture what is known as a "growth mindset."

This concept arose from outstanding work done by Carol Dweck, a professor of psychology at Stanford University. Her findings, presented in her book *Mindset: The New Psychology of Success*, created an absolute shift in the way we define and understand positive attitudes. Dweck's research focused on children in school environments, but, over time, her groundbreaking ideas have turned out to be useful in just about every context, including organizations and companies.

I have lectured on mindset many, many times. Each time I do so, it elicits an overwhelming response that ranges far beyond the content itself. I've come to expect an extraordinary level of involvement from participants as they become deeply inspired by the subject matter. More than in almost any other workshop—and all of my presentations are designed to facilitate sharing—people tend to open up about themselves and their experiences in their respective organizations when the conversation is centered on this subject.

Dweck's mindset concept is the very definition of a great idea. That is, it's one of those kinds of ideas that, when we hear about it, we immediately ask ourselves, "Why didn't I think of that?" Such ideas seem obvious, self-evident, but they are not.

When applied to work environments, as in my workshops, Dweck's concepts help people understand what is happening within their organizations on a day-to-day basis. Just as we ourselves each have a mindset, every company, too, has its own mindset. The latter—which, as we will see, is a direct byproduct of its people's mindsets—is what is typically framed or expressed as the culture of the organization. Usually, organizations define their culture and then disseminate that definition, in the expectation that employees will live by the tenets and values they are presented with. In reality, a culture is defined by what actually happens on a daily basis in the organization. A given company's culture or mindset is not necessarily what those in leadership who came up with the definition think it should be. It's what employees really breathe, what they truly think and talk about, what they live every day.

Just as every company's mindset will produce different results, each of Dweck's mindsets has a completely different outcome. Luckily, her model provides the tools to understand which behaviors will lead everyone to move forward and which will create roadblocks in development, both at the company and individual levels.

Your Abilities Are Not Fixed

Before I dive into Dweck's model during my mindset presentations, I like to start by helping the audience get a sense of the assumptions we all make—and the mindsets that are associated with those assumptions. First, I ask the participants to break into small groups to discuss two specific topics. The first is IQ: is it a fixed factor, or can it be changed? And the second topic is talent: can people increase their level of a given talent or not?

It's fascinating to observe how, when challenged to put their underlying ideas into words, people in my workshops can have such widely varying perceptions of these two concepts. Most of the time, they actually take a contradictory stance, simultaneously framing talent and IQ as unchanging while acknowledging the value and necessity of practice and hard work. Nonetheless, in general, people do believe that someone's IQ is a fixed value that cannot be changed. Once we know our score through a test, we know our permanent IQ. That is, we can expect to receive roughly the same score for the rest of our life. People's beliefs also fall along the same lines regarding talent.

Alfred Binet and Théodore Simon, the creators of the IQ test, administered it for the first time in Paris in 1904. Lewis Terman—like Dweck, a psychologist from Stanford—introduced his version in the United States in 1916. It's important to note that Terman had different intentions than Binet and Simon: he wanted to demonstrate the inborn and unchangeable qualities of intelligence. That, in fact, was the opposite of what Binet and Simon wanted to accomplish. Binet had observed that Parisian children who were performing below average in the traditional education system would be taken out of regular classrooms and permanently moved into classrooms intended for "low-capability" children. He was convinced that what we now call IQ changes over time *if* we (and, often, those who are teaching, raising, and or leading us) invest targeted and regular efforts in that direction. So, he developed his famous test to prove that hypothesis and change the way schools were approaching education for all students. Here was his belief in his own words:

> A few modern philosophers assert that an individual's intelligence is a fixed quantity, a quantity which cannot be increased. We must protest and react against this brutal pessimism. With practice, training, and above all, method, we manage to increase our attention, our memory, our judgement, and literally to become more intelligent than we were before.

Unfortunately, over time—certainly in large part because of Terman's influence—the popular current understanding of IQ as fixed took root. So much so that many otherwise knowledgeable, informed people now think of IQ test results as both definitive and undeviating over a person's lifetime. I consider myself a very open-minded person, yet I'd always thought of the IQ test as something that gave us information about ourselves based on a traditional definition of unchangeable, innate intelligence. You know, either you are intelligent... or you are not. This duality is quite far from what we understand today about intelligence—not to mention what Binet intended!

When I challenge my audience regarding their understanding of the IQ concept—specifically, whether it is fixed or can change—I always encounter the two aforementioned perspectives. True, the vast majority of people initially express the opinion that an IQ score is something that cannot be changed, with just a few positing the potential for variation over time. But once I start pushing against the majority conception, those who believed the former immediately begin to question themselves, and realize that, as with many other aspects of human beings, IQs can and do change over time. So it's not so much that people don't understand that we are able to change, improve, grow. The problem lies in the fact that, without our conscious intervention, the prior—more widespread, dominant, conscious—perspective plays an outsized role in shaping how we think and behave.

After this, we discuss talent along the same lines. Much as the mainstream frames IQ as set and inborn, talent is also typically understood as something inherent, immutable. The general idea of "talented people" frames talent as a fixed factor. That person is talented... and this person is not.

Which individuals do we call "talented"? What are their talents about, exactly? Most of us knew someone in high school or college who seemed remarkably talented. We fully expected that person to be incredibly successful in life. Quite often, once we see how that person's life actually evolved, we realize that—for whatever reason—their talent (or perhaps it's better to say their *potential* talent) never developed. And many of us have encountered the opposite situation, in which people seen as less promising, less talented, or even untalented go on to become very successful in some area of life.

The fact of the matter is that, in most cases, it's impossible to predict if a person is going to be successful in life or not, regardless of whether or not that individual has any kind of visible, recognizable, and/or celebrated talent. There are many true stories of people who ultimately excelled when nobody would have predicted it.

Take the fascinating example of Elon Musk. He was such an undistinguished student throughout elementary and high school in South Africa that one of his teachers said nobody believed he was going to do anything in life. He was also often bullied in his younger years. Yet, nowadays, he is changing the world!

Richard Branson, who is dyslexic and often says he is not at all good with numbers, was able to build an empire of more than two hundred companies. J.K. Rowling's first manuscript was rejected twelve times by several publishing houses, yet once she got it through, her Harry Potter series became a worldwide bestselling franchise—and now she's among the wealthiest people in the U.K.

And, like with Musk, Albert Einstein's teachers didn't think much of him. All the same, he's been our go-to person when discussing genius ever since he won the Nobel Prize a century ago. And this is just scratching the surface. As you can see, it's hard, even impossible, to predict what a person can eventually achieve or develop into throughout their lives.

Does your team, your "talent," have the capacity to grow? That in large part will depend on you. How you approach the distinction between what is possible and what is not has extraordinary implications for leadership. There is no way to nurture people's development or to empower them to shine unless you believe that IQ and talent can be improved.

The Power of Nurture

Now that we understand this concept and its impact on our work as leaders, let's introduce another component: the environment. We'll start by taking a closer look at the eternal nature/nurture argument. This underlying distinction resonates throughout any discussion of mindset, and indeed, throughout our mindsets themselves. That means it needs to be tackled head-on.

For many years, the scientific paradigm gave more importance to nature when trying to determine the potential of an individual to develop skills and acquire achievements. And it is an incontrovertible fact that we don't come into this life "naked," metaphorically speaking. In other words, we are not born as a "blank slate." We arrive, newborn, with a massive amount of information inherited from our biological parents and all of their ancestors. Because we can't currently measure or accurately describe this information in its entirety, it appears from our limited perspective to be endless; but it should not be seen as infinite.

Human beings have about 30,000 genes, and the complete set of genes or genetic material present in a human cell or organism is called a genome. Since DNA refers, strictly speaking, to the molecular building blocks of genes, most people are actually referring to the genome when they talk about a given person's DNA. Research into DNA determination and analysis has resulted in a relatively new and highly profitable business sector. The related technologies are mainly used by the general public to learn about where we and our ancestors came from, but such information is a mere fraction of the data that can be found in our genes.

The Human Genome Project, completed in 2003, was one of the most revolutionary scientific projects ever undertaken. Its goal was to identify the composition of the complete human genome. I still remember the newspaper headlines in my native Argentina, a mostly Catholic country where that religion is enshrined in the constitution: this awesome endeavor was announced with the words, "Scientists have finally opened the book of God."

In Argentina's scientific community, our conversation was dominated by an amazing amount of joy, sparked, fundamentally, by hopes that discoveries from this project would enable us to understand, treat, and/or prevent most human diseases. Unfortunately, over the following seventeen years, not much happened in medicine to fulfill our original expectations.

Nonetheless, thanks to the Human Genome Project, the scientific community became increasingly aware of the importance of another factor in the human expression equation. Understanding our genetic information is still an essential component in developing treatments and solutions, but we now know that there's a factor that's just as vital—or even more so: how the environment influences the expression of that genetic information. In other words, the impact of the "nurture" side of things has come to be seen as incredibly important in our lives, even when it comes to our DNA!

In 1942, Conrad Waddington coined the term "epigenetics" ("above" or "on top of" genetics) to refer to external modifications of or influences on our DNA information. In vastly oversimplified terms, these factors can "turn" genes "on" or "off." Many decades later, ever-mounting evidence shows that environmental and lifestyle factors drive epigenetic mechanisms. In other words, environmental influences are crucial to our lives insofar as how our unique genetics develop, are expressed, and evolve over time. A person could have a genetic predisposition for a certain disease—let's say lung cancer (that is, she has an oncogene for lung cancer)—but if her environment and/or lifestyle don't feed that condition, it's very unlikely that she will end up developing that disease.

And guess what? Epigenetics operate similarly for those genetic predispositions that influence our neurology and, eventually, our mindset. That is, we know from the science behind epigenetics that our environments and we ourselves can play a decisive role in shaping these key elements of who we are.

So, understanding this concept is essential for leaders who want to become active participants in determining how their life is going to progress. Thanks to epigenetics, and to the related, similarly supple capacities of IQ and talent, we have way more power over how our lives unfold than we previously thought. Can we have 100 percent control? The answer is a resounding no. But, with the right approach, we can gain substantial personal power—and accomplish far more in the business realm—by promoting thoughts, habits, and behaviors that foster dynamic, constructive growth mindsets in ourselves and others.

It seems almost unnecessary to state that our attitudes, intelligence, and talents affect actions, and thus outcomes, in a positive or a negative way. Yet we often limit ourselves by failing to take the malleability of these qualities into account, mindlessly accepting basic assumptions about ourselves and others. The latest neuroscience, while aware that there must be some finite aspects, sees the potential of the human brain as virtually limitless!

As I see it, our main mission as human beings is to keep investigating those potential limits. In other words, we have an implicit obligation to explore in ourselves just how far we can go, how much we can grow. In this way, we can all contribute our grain of sand to the science of human potential.

Now that we've dipped into these topics, what do you think about our brains' potential capacities, whether we are talking about IQ, talent, or genetics and epigenetics? With all that I've learned, and all the great information that's coming out, the original motto of the Olympic Games—"faster, higher, stronger"—comes to mind. New records are achieved in every Olympic season, despite prior records that may have seemed unsurmountable. If this can happen through the way we manage our bodies—a part of ourselves we know much more about—how can we limit ourselves with this mysterious organ that surprises us every day? As comedian Don Ward famously said, "If you're going to doubt something, doubt your limits."

Defining Mindset

In this context, a mindset can be defined as an established set of attitudes held by a person or a group. Mindsets include mental habits shaped by experience. When we talk about such habits, it's important to note that we are also talking about beliefs about ourselves and/or others and/or the way the world works.

When we frame our mental habits as based on such beliefs, we are faced with one especially useful and concrete implication: our mental habits are a choice, and, therefore, can be changed.

In the words of motivational speaker and writer Denis Waitley, author of *The New Psychology of Winning*, "It's not who you are that holds you back, it's who you think you are not."

How often do we attempt a specific activity that we've never tried or practiced, only to find that, with time and effort, we become better and better? Any endeavor approached with diligence and consistency will reap some rewards, however small or negligible; some people's exertions will even develop into expertise, renown, and so on. In other words, we are potentially capable of excellence in many situations that we have yet to be exposed to.

Dweck's *Mindset* gives us a brilliant key to accessing that excellence via our mental habits and attitudes. Her work was carried out almost exclusively with children in the school environment, while my work focuses on how her findings and concepts correlate with and apply to organizations and business environments, that is, on human behaviors in the workplace.

In her research, Dweck observed clear and notable differences in the way children tended to face new challenges and problems. In particular, she noticed two distinct modes of behavior when individual children or their classmates made mistakes or faced negative outcomes in their schoolwork. Further, she posited that these action modes stemmed from underlying attitudes. Based on her observations, she defined two specific attitudes: the fixed mindset (FM) and the growth mindset (GM).

Interestingly, characteristics of both are shared by all human beings. There is no one person who is 100 percent growth mindset or 100 percent fixed mindset.

Every human being has these two opposing voices inside, ensconced in a sort of permanent confrontational mode. Fixed mindset mode is more judgmental. It reminds us of our limitations, and results in the type of thinking wherein we believe it will be impossible to make things better or stop repeating a mistake. Growth mindset, on the other hand, encourages us to look for progress and possibility. It helps us focus mainly on improvement and solutions. In the end, the inner mindset you heed the most will become your predominant way of operating in the world. The choice is yours.

Let me reinforce the following concept: our brains have a basic need to make sense about ourselves and others, and the way they do so is by ascribing labels, thereby judging, mainly in a binary (good/bad, safe/dangerous) way. That is to say, most of our five brains spend lots of energy seeking to categorize all input in the clearest and most precise way possible. They are intensely opposed to uncertainty.

We also know, however, that life is not a succession of binary events. Business environments continually pose threats to the reptilian brain and our fear circuitry in the form of unexpected events, ongoing changes, intricate scenarios, complex choices, subtle human dynamics, and more. We've worked so far to build skills in circumventing and training our fear circuitry; through the rest of this chapter, we are going to cast a wider, deeper net, addressing the all-encompassing, underlying mental attitudes that shape our very way of being.

As I delve into this topic, you'll notice that your brains will be constantly trying to judge themselves: Am I a fixed mindset or a growth mindset brain? Growth is better, right? So I must be a GM brain! On the other hand, I make mistakes... so I must be FM! It will go on and on.

Do not be deceived by this totally natural brain bias. Be as objective as you can with what you read, and you will eventually see how the two mental states are both clearly present and active in our lives. Your current mindset depends at any given moment on your particular situation—and even on your mood. No human being is entirely locked into a fixed or growth mindset at all times. We are all constantly moving between these two lenses when looking at the world and attempting to understand it.

True, some people predominantly experience and express one mindset or the other. However, even in such cases there is always a moment—be it through a certain set of circumstances or a specific scenario—when we have the opportunity, and perhaps the impetus, to switch to the opposite mindset. Of course, I don't ever advocate for shifting to a fixed mindset. In both business and personal life, a growth mindset is always more conducive to positive progress. But how do we get there?

Switching Mindsets

Are you aware of how pervasive and tenacious FMs are in most cultures and in our own internal dialogues? One very simple belief can derail an individual's entire existence. This basic yet remarkably destructive belief can be expressed in a single sentence: "Everything should come naturally to me." This way of thinking is a terrible trap, as it places us in the wrong position if we ever want to truly succeed. Yet, to be honest, I cannot deny that I can hear my inner FM voice whispering this to my mind quite frequently. Can't you?

What we forget is that most of those characteristics that we call natural today were not part of our capacities earlier in life. For every skill or talent we may possess, there was an extended period during which we developed the necessary knowledge and abilities, a learning curve, that lasted until the moment in which that activity became natural, known, even effortless. There was always, always a process involved, a time of training and discovery—regardless of IQ, talents, and so on.

We adults tend to forget this incontrovertible fact, and instead expect instant mastery of, well, everything. The risk in accepting "everything should come naturally to me" as a fact—something all of us do sometimes—resides in the way it leaves no room for the possibility that we can progress or get better. When we think everything should come naturally right from the outset, we block any possibility of improvement. Various permutations of this sentiment fuel poor performance and engagement in our personal lives and careers alike.

On the individual level, we stunt our human potential when we think this way; in the workplace, such beliefs can have far-reaching repercussions for employees throughout the organization. But tackling this bastion of FM thinking, along with similar limiting ideas, is totally feasible. With the right tools, you can render GM thinking the dominant, pervasive attitude for you and, eventually, your organization.

Big surprise: switching mindsets is not something that "comes naturally"—it takes effort and practice and intention. More specifically, though, how can we do better? The best way to become proficient in shifting from one mindset to the other is by building self-awareness. We can do this by paying attention to and learning to understand our own internal dialogues. We need to learn the characteristics and patterns of these two inner voices as they occur inside of each of us. Those of us who prefer to shape our destiny rather than unconsciously remain at the mercy of whatever mindset happens to prevail must strive to become masters in identifying instances and qualities of these two different languages through observing and monitoring ourselves.

This is not necessarily a simple process, since each mindset may appear in a range of forms. Our critical, pessimistic, even hopeless fixed mindset, for example, can be hidden in so many taken-for-granted societal and personal assumptions. How do we identify the many different disguises a fixed mindset attitude may wear? We will come back to this question once we've explored both mindsets more thoroughly.

Recognizing the Differences between FM and GM

Let's begin our investigation of these two states by using key words or situations to reveal how an individual expressing each mindset would typically respond.

For instance, take *intelligence.* An individual experiencing/ expressing a fixed mindset will consider intelligence to be something that can't be changed, and will believe that IQ is a fixed factor in the equation of human behavior and success. An individual experiencing/expressing a growth mindset will be convinced that intelligence can be developed, nurtured, worked for, changed.

And what about the concept of *change*? For the FM, change is not exactly appealing. It mainly triggers fear and resistance, because it implies the almost definite possibility of looming uncertainty. A GM, on the other hand, posits that change is the only way to move forward. Someone operating from a GM will therefore embrace change, and be ready for transformation at all times.

Each mindset also interprets the concept of *effort* in a completely different way, based on its own understanding of performance. A person in whom a fixed mindset is dominant will be convinced that intelligence and talent are set, and, therefore, that no amount of effort will better one's performance. They see improvement as, quite simply, an impossible proposition. A person with a predominant GM attitude believes in getting better, and knows that the only way to move forward is to keep making an effort. Moreover, they are convinced that their success depends on—or at least heavily relies on—effort.

Another big distinction between these two mindsets involves their positions regarding *receiving feedback*.

The FM-driven person feels threatened by feedback. They predominantly focus on its negative aspects, and see it as highlighting their mistakes and what they cannot do. Thus, feedback seems to reveal areas of weakness, ways in which they are lacking talent and/or intelligence. On the other hand, a GM-driven individual is always looking for feedback because they're convinced that it will help them grow, develop new skills, and achieve progress and results.

Similarly, *stretch goals* don't work for an FM, but are very encouraging for a GM.

When it comes to *other people's success*, we can see how an FM tends to compare themselves, in order to discern what they haven't done or cannot do as well as others: "They are successful in such and such a way, and I'm not." They look at others through a lens of negative comparison, and so perceive others' success as a largely negative thing. For a GM person, however, successful people offer positive learning opportunities. The GM thinks, "I'm able to be better at what I'm doing when I see and learn about what others have done."

Mistakes are a big challenge for an FM person. They are always read as evidence that they are not good enough. Therefore, FMs avoid admitting their mistakes to themselves and others, and thus generally don't learn from mistakes. A GM knows that mistakes are a doorway to understanding how to do things correctly the next time. In addition to better understanding and performance, the GM approach to mistakes facilitates many pro-social qualities, such as humility, patience, and the propensity for taking restorative action.

FMs perceive whatever they are facing as a threat. The characteristics of their inner thoughts revolve around inability and failure:

- "What if I'm not good enough?"
- "Maybe I don't have the skills for that."
- "I better not try—I could make mistakes."
- "Others may do it better."

GMs see whatever they are facing as a challenge. Their inner thoughts are centered on potential and possibility:

- "I can get better."
- "I can always improve."
- "What a chance to develop skills!"
- "A year ago, I wouldn't have done it this well."

The essence of the GM approach can be summed up in the common saying, "Smart is something you get, not something you are." This amazing, game-changing phrase defines intelligence as a process and not a fixed situation. That's not how we typically think about being smart, right? And yet the science around neurology, the IQ, epigenetics, and related subjects increasingly demonstrates that when we change what we do, we change what we *can do*.

At its root, our mindset is what determines whether we decide such changes are possible and rewarding—or not. Deploying a growth mindset in our thoughts and actions will ensure we take advantage of the near-limitless capabilities of our remarkable human brains.

MINDSET TRANSLATION

We all evince qualities of both mindsets at different times and under different circumstances. You can begin to cultivate a growth mindset by, first, building awareness of your internal dialogue and, second, consciously replacing FM thoughts and habits with those that reflect a GM. Even if you typically tend more toward a GM, you'll benefit from reinforcing that stance. These two exercises will gradually get your brains habituated to and oriented toward GM beliefs, thoughts, and actions.

EXERCISE 1: Moving from a Fixed to a Growth Mindset

STEP 1: Make a simple chart with two columns: FM and GM.

STEP 2: Every time you catch yourself operating from an FM state, distill the underlying idea into a sentence or two and record it in the FM column.

STEP 3: Using what you know of the GM state, and referring back to this chapter if helpful, translate the FM statement into GM language and sentiments, and record it in the second column. For example, if you've written "I never meet my deadlines" in column one, you might write, "If I get more organized and work harder, I'll be able to meet my deadlines." Note that even positive statements can reflect a (more hidden) FM. Take "I'm great at delegating." This attitude implies that you are inherently and already "talented" at this crucial ability. It assumes you don't have more to learn, and leaves you vulnerable to mishandling mistakes and investing minimal effort, as we discussed. In such cases, try replacing judgment with inspiration: "I value delegating and will strive to cultivate great delegation skills."

STEP 4: Repeat the GM sentence to yourself several times. Again, by replacing negative self-talk and attitudes with positive, we are creating and strengthening positive neural patterns. Practice this exercise for at least a few days, until it starts to feel ingrained. Once you've observed yourself developing an ability to catch yourself in FM patterns and replace them with GM ones, you've likely begun to nurture a deep mental habit of GM. You're thus ready to go on to the next exercise, which brings the GM into action and reflection. (There will be more on this aspect in the next chapter.)

EXERCISE 2: From Translation to Action

STEP 1: Make a new chart, adding two more columns to the ones you made in the first exercise. Label these new columns "actions" and "reflections."

STEP 2: Proceed as in the first exercise, but take the time to first add resulting *actions* (if any) to the appropriate column, and then to record any *reflections* on the feelings, habits, ideas, impacts, and so on arising from the FM and GM in that row.

STEP 3: Feel free to return to earlier FM-to-GM translations if you notice later repercussions.

Do you have a fundamental propensity toward one mindset or the other? Did you find it challenging to turn FM phrases into GM ones? What sorts of benefits did you perceive when you replaced FM approaches with more positive, growth-oriented attitudes and actions?

TO CREATE AN ATMOSPHERE IS TO EXPERIENCE THE IMPACT OF AN ESTABLISHED/PERFORMANT MINDSET.

7

Leading with Your Most Productive Mindset

O NCE YOU'VE seen the effectiveness of neuroscience-based tweaks firsthand and reflected on the inner attitude that best supports such advances, you'll inevitably want to extend those benefits to your workplace leadership. Since growth mindsets (GMs) consistently produce exceptional results, the outcome for all concerned may well exceed your expectations.

Mindset on a group level is atmosphere, (corporate) culture, (workplace) tone, ambiance. Dare to dream that something as intangible, elusive, and desirable as a GM work environment can indeed be shaped by shrewd Five Brain Leadership—and then put those ideas into action. Just as inner attention and active self-awareness allow individuals to gradually develop a stronger growth mindset orientation, those same qualities of attentive observation and conscious practice will foster this positive, productive mindset in the business context.

This chapter will launch you on that corporate GM journey. Let's start with communication. Disrupting entrenched ways of interacting facilitates fresh, more fruitful means of working together. And it starts by simply recognizing current tendencies. As we practice conscious, strategic reflection, our actions—including communication—can come to reflect an increasingly positive, proactive underlying stance.

To move forward, it will be useful to take a deeper look at the communication modes associated with the two mindsets we discussed in the previous chapter. What are the usual narratives or dialogues that characterize each attitude? How do they tend to communicate in the work environment? Learning to recognize key words, phrases, and viewpoints that represent each mindset's communication modes helps us extrapolate Carol Dweck's brilliant findings to our own teams and business environments. With this knowledge, we can develop practical, progress-oriented approaches that foster better interactions for all concerned.

[margin note: GROWTH MINDSET.]

Once we understand and accept that we all experience both mindsets, we can naturally begin to identify which of them is being expressed—and is therefore in control—in our way of communicating at any given moment. Remember, too, that our communications elicit specific responses in others. That is, our words (whether spoken, written, even *implied*...) determine and generate behaviors. While a closely linked reaction is not inevitable, we humans are in general more reactive than proactive, and this—along with mirror neurons and other subtle factors—renders a similarly toned response more likely. Thus, if my boss speaks to me from a fixed mindset (FM), I will probably respond, and then act, from the same mindset. In the same way, when I speak from a specific mindset, I will typically engender responses that will resonate in that same frequency.

[handwritten note: THE WAVES WE PUT OUT ARE THE FREQUENCY OTHERS WILL TUNE INTO.]

Those FM interactions can limit us more than we might realize. For example, they're often associated with a helpless, passive "victim" mentality, in which an individual communicates from a perspective that both seeks and expects someone else to save them (just as that stance typically also blames others for past outcomes). In fact, any instance of this mode of communication is a good way to quickly identify an FM-driven inner voice. The assumption is that some other person will solve my challenges, my problems, my life; in other words, that they will do for me anything I am unable to easily, instantly, "naturally" do. Wrong! Danger! Unproductive! ... Totally FM!

To be clear, when we use the word "victim," we're not talking about people who are the victim of very real injustice or abuse. Following Stephen Karpman's "drama triangle" model, I'm referring to the psychologically useless and evasive stance of individuals who (consciously or unconsciously) choose to act out these limiting roles.

What complicates this scenario is that there are many people who feel extremely comfortable in the savior, or in Karpman's terms, "rescuer" role. These individuals are always—usually unconsciously—looking for people who "play victim" in order to exercise their role as saviors. This codependent, self-perpetuating victim-savior circle is totally useless and unproductive. No personal growth or real results can occur when this circuit is activated. Instead, an FM mentality is in play... and in complete control.

In the workplace, this victim-savior dynamic plays out quite frequently between leadership and employees. Those managers who believe they should have all the answers and solutions to problems that arise in their area of responsibility are more likely to slip into a fixed mindset and pass that attitude on to their team. Such presumed omniscience also leads to an authoritarian managerial style.

Unstoppable
Neobuler
nervous
Describer

The paradox here is that authoritarian savior-managers expect employees to be proactive, make their own decisions, and propose solutions, when in fact they themselves push their people in exactly the opposite direction—that is, toward a fixed mindset. What such leaders really want is to maintain absolute control, because that is the only position in which they feel safe. Their unconscious intentions thus collide with what they've been trained to expect from their employees. That is to say, what they've learned in business schools or in leadership trainings is directly at odds with what their personalities are really capable of expressing or putting into practice. Let's keep in mind, however, that unless these leaders are somehow working on themselves—through a coaching process or something similar—it's almost impossible for them to recognize this pattern. Yes, the level of self-deception prevalent among top professionals would astonish you.

Now that we've introduced some typical FM communication styles and discussed their negative impacts, you're probably quite eager to make the switch to GM-style interactions. It will nonetheless remain helpful to bear the pitfalls of FMs in mind as we begin to focus more on actively developing a healthy GM in the work environment. In the sections that follow, we will compare the two. What are the typical narratives of an employee or a manager with an FM or with a GM? How do organizations look, behave, and build their culture from one or the other state of mind?

FM and GM Narratives

How can we recognize each mindset in our employees? Through astute observation. We must discern the underlying attitudes of the people on our team—not only insofar as those attitudes are reflected in how they talk, but also in how they behave in their daily work. Together, words and behaviors reflect one communication style or the other. Certain fundamental narratives shape both the ways employees interact and the ensuing actions—or lack thereof—associated with those stances. Since it is the FM we want to dispel, we must in effect immerse ourselves in that mentality so as to become ineluctably familiar with the very thing we want to transform. As we consider the daunting array of FM statements and attitudes I am about to describe, remember that for each there is a strong and valuable GM antidote.

[handwritten margin note: WHICH PAPER?]

According to a paper by Chris Miller, a program director at UNC Kenan-Flagler, employees operating from an FM narrative will typically:

- **Get defensive.** "Why are you attacking me?" Every comment they receive will be perceived in a negative way. Further, they'll try to avoid accountability. Have a challenge or problem? It's not their fault—nor is it their responsibility to address.

- **Give up easily.** "It didn't come easily to me, so I didn't keep trying." They'll operate from the idea that if they failed the first time, that means they don't have the right skills. And they won't try again, because that sort of effort makes no sense to them.

- **Tend to blame others.** This is the clearest and most representative attitude of an FM mentality. Someone else is always responsible for any and all mistakes and should be blamed for whatever has gone wrong. They are experts at passing the buck. Their mantra is: "It was not my fault"—stated while pointing at others, of course.

- **Cover up their failings.** Remember: their goal is that nobody will realize that they are not capable of doing absolutely every aspect of their job perfectly. Therefore, when mistakes are made, they try to sweep them under the rug.

- **Avoid talking about mistakes.** As above.

- **Avoid challenges.** "That doesn't seem like a good idea." Or "a good fit," or something similar. From an FM perspective, any challenge means exposing yourself to the risk of failure and confirming the self-fulfilling prophecy that you are not smart enough or don't have the necessary talent for the job.

- **Lie about their achievements.** The FM mode doesn't care about the truth, only about image. Employees operating from this attitude need to look competent no matter what.

- **Believe cheating is an option.** For reasons similar to those outlined in the previous trait.

- **Plateau early and fail to achieve their full potential.** Once an FM-driven employee is ensconced in their position, they'll tend to stick with the status quo. This is because things like going the extra mile or taking on a new task are risky.

- **Say, "That's not in my job description."** I'll bet you've heard this sentence before. The FM narrative–driven employee sees their job itself as fixed and inflexible, entailing only certain roles and duties and no others.

- **Believe, "The organization has always done it in the same way, so why change now?"** Another cliché ... but a real issue with this mindset. And a way to avoid learning additional skills, innovating, or trying anything new.

The list could go on and on. I'm sure at this point you will be able to identify other narratives expressed and acted upon by FM employees.

Each of these narratives can be effectively countered from a more productive perspective. For instance, a GM-based leader's response to "That's not in my job description" could be "Then find out whose job description it *is* in," or "What a great opportunity to grow. Learn something new and then you will be able to include it in your job description!" Or, if faced with a team member who wants to do things "the way they've always been done," try deflecting this worn-out excuse with words such as ("We are just learning one more way to do it.")

What happens when the FM employees concerned are managers—leaders of teams and organizations with wide-ranging responsibilities? What are some typical narratives expressed by managers operating from an FM?

FM narrative–driven managers often:

- **Fail to recognize positive changes in employee performance.** Their approach entails making everyone on their team feel subtly—yet permanently and inevitably—inept, as they believe this stance is the best way to keep control.

- **Believe development is a waste of time and money.** "Everyone should know what they must do, that's why I hired them." Managers operating from an FM narrative feel they are not responsible for employee development. In fact, they think, "If they don't know how to do their job, I don't need them."

- **Emphasize hierarchy in groups.** FM-driven managers rely on hierarchies in a negative way: "I am the boss," "I decide, and you execute," "I am in control." They don't ask for suggestions or proposals, and always have to have the last word. They need to show that they're the boss at all times, because honoring others' suggestions and proposals means losing power, and thereby becoming weak, disrespected, and so on. They cannot show vulnerability!

- **View any failing by their employees as emblematic of low intelligence or incompetence.** "Team members should know what to do all the time, period."

- **Are less likely to coach employees about how to improve performance or to offer constructive feedback.** For all the obvious reasons, FM-based managers don't value coaching or feedback. Moreover, they don't know how to act as a coach for team members, or how to proactively, constructively, helpfully critique them. They see the world in a binary way: "Either you know, or you don't." There is no room for improvement; there are no gray areas in which to search and strive for new skills and knowledge.

Now let's delve into how leaders and employees communicate when they are approaching their work from a GM point of view. What are the narratives of an employee who is predominantly functioning from a growth-oriented state of mind? One way to figure this out would be to simply translate each of the FM narratives I just listed into GM language and meanings.

For instance, while an FM employee might reason that something "didn't come easily" so they stopped trying, a GM employee will think: "I'll keep trying until I succeed" or even, "I'll try a new, different approach." Where an FM-driven employee might get defensive or cover up their mistakes, a GM-driven employee will be receptive to constructive criticism and take steps to learn from their mistakes.

The FM-based manager who believes "team members should know what to do all the time, period," has their GM counterpart in the manager who believes "team members can always learn more about anything." And whereas the former will tend to assert dominance and control laden with expectations of perfection, the latter will be open to suggestions from the entire team, and will be ready to delegate, not to mention offer resources for development and improvement over past performance. Bottom line: when compared to any FM narrative, a GM essentially engenders the opposite response.

Your Brain Loves to Make Mistakes

To understand why the contrast is so stark, it will be helpful to discuss what happens in our brain when we make mistakes in what we feel to be a safe environment. Recent neuroscience findings show that under such conditions our brain will activate (or "turn on") the centers used for learning. When this happens, we are able to more quickly form new neural connections, even as we learn to fix those mistakes with new knowledge, skills, and/or tactics. In other words, when we make mistakes, and then find ways to amend them, in a non-threatening environment, we can learn faster, and therefore grow our brainpower—all the while furthering our goals!

As we know, the brain creates new neurons all the time. For each of our thoughts and actions, the brain generates a net of connections among neurons. Each neuron has at least 10,000 connections. Each neuron, by itself, is not worth much. Instead, the value of all of our neurons relies on the power of their connections. Like people, our neurons grow in capacity through their relationships with each other.

When we make a mistake—again, in a workplace (or other environment) that feels safe—our brain is eager to find the solution and will open itself completely to the experience of gaining new and better skills and information. Eager to connect, our whole fabulous, five-part brain and its amazing learning centers will deploy all the necessary neurons and neural networks for progress.

There is no doubt about it: mistakes, blunders, stumbling blocks, temporary failures, and so on spur learning. As Thomas Edison once said when he was asked why he was still trying to create the lightbulb after so many failures, "I have not failed. I've just found 10,000 ways that won't work." However, this type of enhanced post-mistake growth is only possible if the organization allows its members to fail without negative consequences.

What we know today is that employees who are predominantly driven by a GM are more likely to seek opportunities for self-improvement and change. And, crucially, failure will not be a barrier to further efforts on their part. The most important consequence of this GM narrative is that such employees will try as many times, and in as many ways, as needed to overcome any obstacle.

This holds true at every level of any enterprise, including the upper echelons. There is a great story about a GM leader at a financial corporation. One of the company's SVPs made a transaction that caused to the company to lose $10 million. Without hesitation, the SVP went to see his boss, the CEO of the organization, and willingly offered his resignation. The CEO's response was: "Are you crazy? We've just invested $10 million in your training and development! How can you even think we are going to let you go? No way! Now, let's discuss what you learned, and what you are planning to do to recover the money."

A similar approach comes from a well-known telecommunication company that decided to establish a bonus for "mistakes." Whenever an employee proved that they were pushing the boundaries through their bold ideas, they received a bonus... even if their invention or innovation didn't work at all!

One of the reasons so many people want to work at Google is because the organization's leadership is very keen to cultivate a learning culture. A main goal is to provide employees with the right information that they will need on the job. They also encourage employees to create a treasure trove of knowledge that is then made available and easily accessible to the rest of the company. Basically, Google tries to exponentially multiply the learning curve—and thereby multiply results. Arguably, the key aspect of their learning culture has nothing to do with information. Instead, Google's remarkable productivity and innovation may well depend most on the corporation successfully creating an atmosphere in which everyone feels safe asking questions and sharing their ideas.

Companies that do learning culture right know that it's not just about learning. As recruitment and development expert Josh Bersin says, "the learning curve is the earning curve." Or, in the words of Tala A. Nabong, "Learning cultures improve employee engagement, lower turnover, improve employee satisfaction, encourage problem solving among employees, and increase employee retention."

The deeper meaning of a growth mindset remains elusive for some. *Harvard Business Review* lays out some common misconceptions or myths, including the notion that the GM is:

- **Unbounded.** This is unrealistic. We need to learn how to deal with both mindsets, as well as how to tip the scales toward the predominance of a growth mindset.

- **Binary.** Assuming that mental states are binary, and that we can only be one or the other, is one of the most frequent mistakes made around mindset. Normally, our minds oscillate between the two. Our job is to clearly identify which one is speaking at any given moment—and act accordingly.

- **Reflected by a positive attitude, no matter what.** This is one of the greatest human fantasies: thinking that we can stay positive, regardless of circumstances, all the time. Our emotions behave like ocean tides, with cyclical, inevitable highs and lows, along with in-between and transitional periods. Indeed, these changes are, paradoxically, how we maintain balance. Learning how to surf our tidal emotional patterns is where the secret lies.

- **Possessed by any given business.** Definitely not! Businesses in themselves are neutral. Our intervention gives them a positive or negative culture, meaning, and so on.

So, having a growth mindset doesn't necessarily mean possessing a totally positive outlook, or even being flexible and open-minded all the time. Yes, these characteristics are generally desirable, but since everyone actually has a mixture of fixed and growth mindsets it's unrealistic to expect constant expression of one "right" attitude. In reality, each individual's mixture continuously evolves with their knowledge, intentions, and experience.

Returning to the narratives of employees with a GM, let's look into a five-year study Dweck and others carried out in various organizations. Their main conclusions touched upon differences between mindsets in the workplace. When compared to peers expressing an FM, GM employees are more likely to:

- Say their colleagues are **trustworthy**
- Express a **strong sense of ownership and commitment** to their organizations
- Believe their company supports **risk-taking**
- State that their organization fosters **innovation**

Furthermore, they found that managers operating predominantly from a GM...

- **Surround themselves with able and talented people because they do not feel threatened by them.** They know that success is based on hiring the best people—despite the possibility that such hires might eventually or in some regards do better than they themselves could. They understand that their role involves helping the individuals on their team reach the best possible version of themselves in order to achieve superior results. A GM-driven manager's role is equivalent to that of an orchestra conductor: they know that they don't need to be proficient in every single instrument, but they are experts on how those many instruments should be combined to achieve the best performance possible. And, like a conductor, they understand that they shine through their people's success.

- **Forecast the resources that they and their people will need in the future.** Success doesn't only involve already-present skills, information, and so on. GM managers plan out what each team member needs to develop and move to their next level of mastery. With those resources available, each individual can give even more of themselves to achieve the best results.

- **Reward efforts, not just outcomes.** Both in my experience as a coach and in my research, I've found that acknowledging individual and team achievements is not a customary practice. "Consider your salary as recognition of your work" seems to be the most common narrative among leadership. This is a big mistake. It's a little better—but still not ideal—for managers to simply recognize employees when results are achieved. In contrast, managers with a GM understand that acknowledging and celebrating the process of striving for results is even more important. This approach makes a far greater impact on employee attitudes because it supports vital learning practices. Not only do such employees produce positive results, they also learn that sincere and diligent efforts are rewarded, worthwhile, effective.

- **Make better negotiators, and look for win-win deals.** The GM manager understands that a truly successful negotiation will generate a long-term business relationship. Therefore, they always seek to close agreements in such a way that both parties win.

- **Enable their organizations to build a GM culture that is inherently more collaborative and innovative.** Such a culture is a natural consequence in companies led by managers who model and elicit GM narratives, attitudes, and beliefs. GM-driven teamwork is constitutively based on mutual support and encouragement, thereby creating a safe environment for individual and shared efforts, experimentation, and collaboration.

- **Build teams with higher levels of loyalty, motivation, retention, creativity, problem-solving, and cooperation.** A workplace that is flexible, growth-focused, uplifting, and open to imperfection allows our brains to learn and perform better on a variety of levels. This has many interpersonal and corporate repercussions, as reflected in these findings.

It's vital to note one key component that runs through all of these assets: GM-oriented managers realize that, at any given moment, each individual on their team is at their own unique stage of experience and growth, with a different ability level, as well as different distinct strengths and weaknesses currently in play. Therefore, they make it their business to know their people well on an ongoing basis. Their goal is to generate a GM in the team through being proactive in their own development—and sharing the benefits of those efforts with the team in ways that will be useful to each individual member.

Thus, when I coach executives on their leadership capabilities, one of the topics we focus heavily on is how much they know about their people, particularly when it comes to their development. I ask them to define in a very precise way what each of their team members need to learn in order to move to their next level of development. I'm not talking about promotion, but rather about getting better at whatever they already do. In the world of motivational factors, this is known as *mastery*.

Obstacles to a Growth Mindset Culture

How difficult is it to introduce a lasting GM culture into an organization? Well, first of all, we need to admit that doing so can be far from simple, given the entrenched obstacles in most work environments. You will need to craft a thoughtful strategy and implement the entire process wisely, patiently, and carefully, even changing course when necessary to ensure your team's learning culture is as positive and durable as possible.

What are the challenges to creating a permanent learning culture in the organization? Four barriers can mitigate the transformation GM leaders seek. These are biases toward:

- Success
- Action
- Fitting in
- Being experts

Let's look at how each of these biases subtly undermines a growth mentality.

Success

Success is an essential, absolutely necessary component of any business. The problem arises when organizations push the concept of success in the wrong direction, that is, when they demand success everywhere, in every endeavor, every time. In this mode, a bias toward success actually starts playing against results.

Success is a must, but only as the ultimate outcome of work performed over time. Success must occur in—and be framed by leaders as—the result, not the process. During the process itself, we must be allowed to make mistakes, fix them, try again, fail again, and then, *eventually*, find the right ways to achieve our goals.

Those companies that embed success into their processes will create a fixed mindset instead of an open-minded one. In such environments, employees will internalize a narrative that does not encourage innovation, risk-taking, or perseverance, such as, "If I'm not successful at every step of the process, I'm not good enough."

Action

In companies with a bias toward action, there is no time for reflection. We must be doing something all the time. If you imagine you don't have this bias, think again. Have you ever noticed how, when we discuss our day, we always comment about how busy we were? How many things we did—and how much we were not able to finish? Can you imagine saying to your partner or a friend, "I spent two hours just reflecting on a challenge at work today"? They wouldn't even understand what you meant! And if they did believe you, they would think you were procrastinating. In the vast majority of work cultures (and beyond), we must be doing something every waking moment. Either we are taking action or we are "dropping the ball," "lazy," "wasting time," and so on. We have neither time nor permission (implicit or explicit) to simply stop and think as part of the job.

Fitting In

Uniformity plays against innovation and productivity. When we are all are trying to fit in, we are not bringing our own strengths to the job. Our valuable yet different perspectives are missing. Diversity is what triggers new and productive ways of thinking, and, therefore, of doing. It's the only way to learn from each other and to move forward. Yet the FM social/community values of homogeneity and conformity are often deeply integrated into work cultures, even as diversity is given lip service.

Being Experts

This bias entails two different areas of risk. On the one hand, some organizations depend too much on external experts or consultants. In such contexts, employees will typically elect not to step outside of their comfort zone. Somebody else, "the expert," will provide the solution. The narrative here: "Why stretch our minds?"

On the other hand, some companies demand perfection of their experts, whether they are internal or external hires. Managers and employees alike may make the incorrect assumption that "experts don't make mistakes." That's the reason they are experts, after all. Wrong! Experts are exceptionally knowledgeable in their subject. That means they have more resources to solve any challenge that may arise in the process, not that they are omniscient and infallible.

Once, while I was presenting this workshop to a consultancy company, the CEO stood up and asked, "What can we do, then? Our company only hires experts. Each employee is an expert in their field." My response was a question: "Do you accept that experts can make mistakes and learn from them?"

Whether the unconscious message is "experts will solve our problems" or "experts don't make mistakes," we are running into a fixed mindset mode.

How to Boost a Growth Mindset in Your Organization

As you invest in getting to know your employees from a perspective of enhancing their development and supporting them as they build mastery, bearing the four key biases we just explored in mind will facilitate surfacing the elements currently most in need of strategic focus. Luckily, leaders who've been practicing GM thinking will enjoy the challenge of initiating and sustaining this worthwhile process. Now, we will investigate some practical steps that can be taken in this direction.

Just as the "fixed" notion of DNA was broken open by the concept of epigenetics, the entrenched FM cultures of organizations can be dispelled by aligning attitudes, narratives, and other factors with a GM perspective—starting at the top. Once again, Dweck shines the light for the path ahead. As mentioned in Chapter 6, Dweck did most of her research in learning institutions, specifically elementary and high schools. She still works mainly with young students. One of her greatest achievements was to introduce a program into those schools that helps children shift from a fixed to a growth mindset.

How can we extrapolate from her student-oriented approach to apply this to people in companies?

First, leaders must understand which mindset is predominant in themselves, both in general and at any given moment—and be able to analyze their own state on an ongoing basis. A critical aspect of this self-awareness is the way leaders understand their own actions and motivations vis-à-vis their employees.

To that end, I would like to propose some helpful questions to ask ourselves from time to time.

Tool: Mindset Questions

In and of themselves, each of these thought exercises can prod your mind to shift its mindset.

- What is my attitude regarding my own mistakes? Am I defensive? Do I learn from my mistakes?

- Do I understand what a learning experience represents for me and for my team? How can I create one?

- Do I really believe that the best way to get results is through my people's development? If I expect excellence, do I provide the tools and encouragement for developing mastery?

- What is my attitude when members of my team question my viewpoints?

- How do I define success? Do I allow space for the all-important yet imperfect process?

- Do I actively build in time and support for reflection? If not, how can I do so? Do I have people on my team who would relish playing a role in furthering this goal?

- Do I truly celebrate differences and diversity? If not, how can I do so? Is there someone on my team who might benefit from the opportunity to help with this?

Leaders must find their own ways to communicate and live their GM. There are many ways to lead a team. And, of course, the unique qualities of each organization necessitate varied approaches to integrating a GM orientation in the workplace. Nonetheless, certain broad parameters—such as the general attitudes of each mindset, and the value of getting to know your employees—as well as some tools, including most of the questions I just listed, hold true for just about every work-place context.

In my work, I've found that many aspects of executive coaching transfer well to the team context. Recent implementation of coaching techniques by savvy leaders has demonstrably impacted results for the better. What do I mean by a coaching-style approach to leadership? Exactly this: a coach-leader will prioritize building trust, ask questions, practice active listening, understand their people's motivations, and work proactively on their people's development. In turn, these foci have a range of positive consequences, including improved engagement and better results.

Since this managerial modality emphasizes collaboration, personal and professional development, and actively creating a supportive environment, leaders who truly comprehend and fully embrace a coaching style in their leadership practices are more likely to develop a team with a growth mindset.

Here are some concrete examples of how to shift our team members from an FM to a GM:

Fixed Mindset	Growth Mindset
Focusing on performance, scores, and judgments	Focusing on how to improve, how to learn more
Primarily praising talent and intelligence	Praising processes, effort, strategy, perseverance
Telling people what to do all the time	Encouraging people to express their insights and cultivate productive habits
Communicating unilaterally and only from the top down	Cultivating an open communication style
Using rankings to judge people, depleting steady confidence	Co-developing areas for growth and mastery, building enduring confidence
Creating dog-eat-dog, hierarchical, competitive, and/or homogeneous environments	Nurturing safe, cooperative, diverse, inclusive, collaborative environments

A fixed mindset says, "It's now or never," reasoning that "If I can't do it now, I don't have enough talent or intelligence, and I will never be able to do it." A growth mindset counters: "Not yet! Maybe I can't do it now, but if I invest more effort, I will be able to do it eventually." The latter perspective fosters a love of learning and boosts resilience—two essential components of great accomplishments.

The reasons for cultivating a GM in personal and professional contexts are abundantly clear. In the words of the sociologist Benjamin Barber, "I don't divide the world into the weak and the strong, or the successes and the failures. I divide the world into the learners and non-learners." And to repeat a very old saying that was popularized by Henry Ford: "Whether you think you can, or you think you can't, you are right."

By definition, learning cultures in the workplace enable employees to "think they can," and they generate a workforce composed of active, confident learners. Such cultures are inevitably helmed by managers who take the time to be self-reflective and who get to know their people well. With targeted efforts, patience, and practice, self-aware leaders can shift themselves and their organizations over to a truly successful, more productive, agile, positive growth mindset.

ORGANIZATIONAL MINDSET CHECKUP

A learning culture is a large-scale, interpersonal growth mindset. Most companies have an entrenched work culture that relies heavily on stated or unstated fixed mindset beliefs. As you embark on your efforts to transition your organization/team to a learning culture, you and your team members will need to play new roles if you want to engender real transformation.

This exercise is intended for leaders and employees alike. It can be done rather formally, as described here, or in a more ad hoc fashion. Once you've had some frank, productive conversations on the benefits of a growth mindset and learning culture—ideally enriched by experienced coaching in this area—your team will be ready to up-level their own environment. So encourage your community to share and follow through on their insights and ideas for great switches with you and with each other.

Over time, it will become natural to support each in this evolving context by talking and listening openly, making and learning from mistakes, and finding new ways to grow together.

EXERCISE: Recognizing FM and GM

In this exercise, you and/or team members will take on a detective role, seeking out fixed and growth mindsets in all their many forms. Then each of you will act as a doctor, finding remedies for the various permutations of fixed mindset thinking you discovered in the previous role (and boosting GM manifestations).

Think of this checkup as an ongoing process, and don't rush into instant solutions. The outcome will be all the richer for allowing a bit of time for your initial findings to "cook" in your brain.

Again, you and/or your team members can follow these steps as laid out, or simply implement this approach casually throughout your day.

STEP 1: First, take an overview of your workspace. Keep your eyes and ears open for evidence of one mindset or the other. This might include anything from information on posters or signs to the way the work environment is set up (think: reception, meeting places, individual work areas, and so on; for those working from home, look for how your furniture is set up, the art or other visual items on display, and so on). Eventually, you might also try to discern disguised messages, such as those purporting to be positive but actually indicative of an FM, for example, "We celebrate our employees' talents!" But start small—aim for one or two specific observations of each mindset, or an assessment of the overall tone.

STEP 2: Next (or another time, or instead . . .), think about what's in your computer. Anything from emails, white papers, or in-progress projects to software, intranet, or workflow platforms could demonstrate—subtly or not-so-subtly—one attitude or the other. (Note: Try to stay open-minded and uncritical as you perform steps 1 and/or 2, bearing in mind all the while that you are looking for opportunities for growth and transformation, not incrimination and judgment.)

STEP 3: Now for your remedial role. Feel free to tackle this part on your own or in collaboration. Think of the instances of FM you have encountered in your team's work environment and/or your personal space, equipment, and/or communications, and then consider these questions:

- What specific underlying narrative drives each such expression?
- What can you learn from your new perspective on this FM manifestation?
- How can you shift the message and attitude expressed therein to reflect a healthier, more productive narrative?
- How can you actively replace FM elements with GM ones?
- And how might you best disseminate this fabulous new GM approach?

STEP 4: Now, think of any examples of a GM. (It wasn't all bad, right?) Where you have detected a GM, can you think of ways to amplify that message?

STEP 5: Finally, and most importantly, a learning culture is built by shared engagement and commitment. Be sure to talk openly with other team members about your process. Solicit their opinions and ideas for further progress toward embracing a learning culture as a team. As we've seen here and in previous chapters, a transparent, inclusive approach to leadership helps the brains of all concerned confidently navigate changes and flourish in every endeavor.

Are You a Biased Leader?

O NE OF the essential characteristics required from leaders is an ability to make decisions. As we well know, the higher a leader is in the organization, the greater the responsibility they have—and the more their decisions will impact many others in quite varied, extensive, and even unexpected ways. Do you think your decisions are affected by your biases? No? Or... not too much? Read on.

In this chapter, we will establish a working definition of, and parameters for, the sorts of biases that impact leadership. You will begin to take stock of how these instantaneous and incredibly subtle processes do in fact shape your perceptions of the world and your decisions more deeply than you ever would have imagined. Then, in the next chapter, we will explore the impacts of biases with an eye toward providing a strong impetus for taking action, and then delve into ways to expand our awareness and transform our actions so as to allow us to sidestep our inevitable unconscious influences.

Leaders face many challenges, but perhaps one of the most important is the need to make decisions under the pressure of urgent deadlines, in times when all of the necessary information is rarely available. An effective leader must have the ability to make crucial choices quickly, in high-intensity, high-stakes environments, with limited knowledge. This distinctive strength is one of the main components of truly successful leadership.

In such moments, leaders must rely on their experience, knowledge, and skills, along with another vital factor that is not always well regarded in the business world: the ability to know how to listen to and adequately decode their gut feelings.

Remember how, in our first discussion of the five brains—in particular about the digestive brain—we learned that what we call our "gut feelings" actually work through algorithms, much like those found in modern technology? This subtle information that we receive and store and refer to as our gut feelings doesn't come from nowhere. It arises out of an elaborate internal process of connecting data that ultimately allows us to arrive at conclusions about people, environments, and situations. So it's basically processed information provided by our gut nervous system.

Now it's time to introduce a "but" about those gut feelings. As you may recall, our five brains include one that's the headquarters of instincts and another that houses emotions. These two brains are addicted to repeating patterns and routines. In essence, that means every challenge that has to be solved will pass through the filter of our past experiences.

And, believe it or not, when we talk about our past experiences we are not referring only to those experiences we've had in our own lives. Our primitive brains carry the experiences of all humankind over many millions of years. These parts of our brains are especially driven by quasi-automated learning ingrained long ago related to our understanding of possible danger and how to defend or protect ourselves. All of that knowledge, which is currently largely unconscious in most of us, has been crucial to keeping us alive. But is it still as useful as before? Not necessarily. At least not all the time.

How can the safety-oriented responses and patterns our brains built up over countless dangerous prehistoric millennia affect our decisions in a negative way today? That is what we are going to discuss in this chapter.

We can start by saying quite simply that the negative influence of these ingrained, non-conscious, and automated patterns results in what we now call biases. Every time we make any decision or arrive at any conclusion, there is a potential risk of being influenced by these outdated patterns.

Rest assured, there are ways to address and even avoid these patterns in order to enhance your leadership skills and decision-making, particularly in the aforementioned high-pressure context. But first you need to hack your own automated systems to begin to figure out and acknowledge how even you—likely a highly educated person with extensive responsibilities and an impressive career—are positively jam-packed with biases. That's where this chapter comes in.

Armed with more information about what shapes your decision-making process, you can learn to rely on less automatic, and more mindful, positive, inclusive, innovative parts of your brains. Over the years, I've developed some good ways to jump-start this process. I always start my workshops on bias by asking the participants to evaluate themselves via a brief test containing ten statements. Participants rate how true each sentence is as applied to themselves or their opinions on a scale of 1 (low agreement) to 5 (high agreement). After taking the test, respondents average their answers to come up with their result. In this way, both they and I gain a better idea of how they perceive themselves.

I invite you to take this test before you continue reading this chapter. It's a good way to assess what and how we think about ourselves.

The Self-Perception Evaluation

This tool is condensed and adapted from David McRaney's brilliant book *You Are Not So Smart*, in which he leads the reader through a journey of unlearning so much of what we all take for granted and think we know.

Rate each of the following ten of McRaney's statements according to how much you agree with them regarding yourself or your opinion on the stated subject, with "1" meaning you strongly disagree and "5" meaning you strongly agree.

1   **"I am a rational, logical being who sees the world as it really is."**

    1   2   3   4   5

2   **"I know when I am being influenced and how it is affecting my behavior."**

    1   2   3   4   5

3   **"I know when I am lying to myself."**

    1   2   3   4   5

4   **"My opinions are the result of years of rational, objective analysis."**

    1   2   3   4   5

5   **"I know why I like the things I like and feel the way I feel."**

    1   2   3   4   5

6 "With the advent of mass media, I clearly understand
how the world works, based on statistics and facts
culled from many examples."

1   2   3   4   5

7 "I prefer the things I own over the things I don't
because I made rational choices when I bought them."

1   2   3   4   5

8 "When I argue, I try to stick to the facts."

1   2   3   4   5

9 "Problems are easier to solve when a group of people
gets together to discuss solutions."

1   2   3   4   5

10 "Wine is a complicated elixir, full of subtle flavors
only an expert can truly distinguish, and experienced
tasters are impervious to deception."

1   2   3   4   5

Now, complete the exercise by adding all of your answers
together and dividing by 10 to calculate your average, which
is your score for the test.

Understanding Your Biases

What was your average result?

In my seminars, participants typically average between
3 and 4.5. Was your result in the same range?

Starting the workshop with this exercise is rather provocative, but it's also super useful because it paints a concrete
picture about how we perceive ourselves and why. And it

makes us think twice about our entrenched beliefs. That's because the "correct" answer is that any result above an average of 1 reflects our biases!

Participants usually don't like hearing this. They don't feel comfortable with my assertion that they "don't know what they know they know." Their faces reflect strong rejection, even anger, as they get into defensive mode to justify and rationalize their results.

I get it. It's not easy to accept that most of our perceptions are based on wrong assumptions. We justify or back up our thoughts by relying on what feels comfortable, grounding them in those expectations and beliefs that come "naturally" to us. We build our reality based on what we feel is right, and not necessarily on what actually is right. In short, we construct our understanding of the world based on concepts that feel natural and come easily to us. But all those appealing qualities do not mean we are correct.

To develop this idea further, we must explore the concept of identity. Our identities form over our entire lifetime, encompassing and integrating everything from our environment and the people around us and shaping what we see as "normal," "desirable," and so on. This phenomenon extends to the formation of our most basic yet deeply rooted ideas about "how the world is," not to mention "who I think I am." The latter helps us understand that we *have* a self—an identity that thinks and acts in certain ways, has certain tastes and preferences, and so on.

Because these beliefs are interconnected, we perceive anything that challenges any of our pervasive assumptions about the external world as threatening to our identity. Since the way I build my reality shapes my identity—who I think I am—anything that shakes this foundation feels dangerous. When my fundamental ideas about how the world works are called into question, I feel I am at risk. I want to stay safe, and I think that the way to do so is to rationally prove, by my own internal logic and belief system, that this new information is incorrect. So that's what most people do when faced with anything that contradicts their assumptions!

But if those assumptions are limiting—and they are— this automatic response limits us even more. The moment our assumptions are "in danger," we have an opportunity to become more agile human beings by working on our own perceptions about our identity. How? With a combination of curiosity, humility, courage, and self-awareness.

In the business environment, this process acquires great importance as far as the way I lead my team, the decisions I make, the impact of those decisions on results, and, especially, what my attitude will be when I see that my decisions are not working as expected or that they differ from others' opinions.

Right after I have thrown the bomb of "all of your percep- tions about yourselves are strongly biased" to my audience, I distribute McRaney's findings for each test statement. In each case there is a heading, representing the type of incor- rect assumption, then a misconception (i.e., the statement itself), and, finally, a clarification, as follows:

1 **Blind Spot Bias**

   The Misconception: You are a rational, logical being who sees the world as it really is.

   The Truth: You are as deluded as the rest of us, but that's OK, it keeps you sane.

2 **Priming**

   The Misconception: You know when you are being influ- enced and how it is affecting your behavior.

The Truth: You are unaware of the constant nudging you receive from ideas formed in your unconscious mind.

3 Confabulation

The Misconception: You know when you are lying to yourself.

The Truth: You are often ignorant of your motivations and create fictional narratives to explain your decisions, emotions, and history without realizing it.

4 Confirmation Bias

The Misconception: Your opinions are the result of years of rational, objective analysis.

The Truth: Your opinions are the result of years of paying attention to information that confirmed what you believed, while ignoring information that challenged your preconceived notions.

5 Introspection

The Misconception: You know why you like the things you like and feel the way you feel.

The Truth: The origins of certain emotional states are unavailable to you, and when pressed to explain them, you will just make something up.

6 The Availability Heuristic

The Misconception: With the advent of mass media, you clearly understand how the world works, based on statistics and facts culled from many examples.

The Truth: You are far more likely to believe something is commonplace if you can find just one example of it, and you are far less likely to believe in something you've never seen or heard of before.

7 Brand Loyalty

The Misconception: You prefer the things you own over the things you don't because you made rational choices when you bought them.

The Truth: You prefer the things you own because you rationalize your past choices to protect your sense of self.

8 The Straw Man Fallacy

The Misconception: When you argue, you try to stick to the facts.

The Truth: In any argument, anger will tempt you to reframe your opponent's position.

9 Groupthink

The Misconception: Problems are easier to solve when a group of people gets together to discuss solutions.

The Truth: Although multiple perspectives do often add to problem-solving capacity, progress is hindered when individuals in groups share a desire to reach consensus and attempt to avoid confrontation.

10 Expectation

The Misconception: Wine is a complicated elixir, full of subtle flavors only an expert can truly distinguish, and experienced tasters are impervious to deception.

The Truth: Wine experts and consumers can be fooled by altering their expectations.

Once I give the participants time to read McRaney's analyses of the ten statements, a debate begins that I find interesting to observe. Despite McRaney's and my convincing assertions, most individuals continue trying to justify their initial observations, their minds hard at work searching for reasons to confirm their self-perceptions in any way possible. Instead of considering the possibility that what we are saying might be true, they keep trying to rationalize their own set ideas and identity.

Aren't we fascinating creatures? Did you know that the feeling of being right activates the reward system in our brains? This is another incredibly significant impetus behind our clinging to our perception of knowing the "right" decision or "fact." Of course, our brains don't want to give up so easily on such a positive emotion! Plus, there's the afore-mentioned impact on our perception of our identity. So, just as we have discussed in previous chapters regarding other topics, there are tremendous neural forces arrayed against changing our minds. As self-aware people interested in personal and professional growth, however, we have to learn to leverage the bigger picture and longer-term rewards to go beyond these limiting base responses.

In my workshops, I usually invest some time in explaining my position, so that most participants are at least able to understand and accept that they are somewhat more biased than they originally believed. How about you? Do you accept that we don't have a completely accurate perception of ourselves?

In some ways, incorrectly perceiving ourselves as objective observers of the world, as logical, rational beings (as in the first statement), is necessary. It allows us to function in our daily lives, and helps us stay sane and move forward in life. So, don't panic! You get to keep some of your illusions.

But let's turn things around so that your identity and perceptions serve you, rather than making you a profoundly biased servant to your automatic assumptions and reactions.

How the Brain Responds to the Outside World

I would like to introduce a way of understanding the functioning of the brain in its interactions with the outside world. To that end, I will start by asking you to solve two math equations. The first one is this:

$$2 + 4$$

How long did it take you to arrive at the result? Almost no time, right? You don't really have to think to solve this equation.

How about when I ask you to solve this one?

$$(687 \times 392)$$

Completely different situation, right? You will likely need to ask me for enough time to do the calculations on paper or to borrow a calculator. You'll definitely have to pull from another area of your brain. Unlike with the first equation, solving this problem does not involve an automatic and easy process.

In fact, through the latter exercise I am literally activating and challenging a completely different part of your brain.

To help us understand how these two different areas of our brain interact with the outside world in our daily life, let's explore Daniel Kahneman's concept of how the brain works. Kahneman, a psychologist and economist, is known for studying the psychology of judgment and decision-making. His work on behavioral economics won the 2002 Nobel Memorial Prize in Economic Sciences.

Kahneman has found that our brain reacts and responds to the external world via two different systems, which he calls System 1 and System 2. In the example with the two math problems, System 1 can quickly address the first equation while System 2 must be activated to solve the second. You can see why from the characteristics Kahneman lists for each system:

System 1	System 2
Fast	Slow
Effortless	Effortful
Uncontrolled	Controlled
No self-awareness	With self-awareness
Automatic	Reflective

In his words, "System 1 is the one that runs the show, that's the one you want to move." Kahneman was one of the first to understand the power, extent, and mechanisms by which our non-conscious mind influences our daily life. His work clearly demonstrates that, unbeknownst to us, System 1 is basically ruling our daily decisions and actions. Our responses to the outside world originate in the parts of our brains that are best suited to certain kinds of situations and not others. Unfortunately, the modern business environment is not the sort of context System 1 should oversee. This is in large part because System 1 is profoundly and inherently and *inevitably* biased.

Where Biases Come From

Let's take a look at the fundamental components of System 1, our biases. You are already an expert on our five different brains, which we broke down in detail in Chapter 1. As we approach the culmination of all we've learned so far, I'm going to build on that knowledge—and specifically on Paul D. MacLean's triune model—to explain on how our brain is structured to favor cognitive biases.

Together, the reptilian brain, where our instincts are located, and the emotional (or limbic) brain host Kahneman's System 1 processes. Our rational brain houses what Kahneman calls System 2. Basically, our biases are located in our reptilian and emotional brains, with the rational brain taking up the rear as the lazy fact checker.

Why does the brain work like this? It's actually quite simple. We know that we are still alive as a civilization thanks to our most primitive brains, mainly the reptilian one. That brain is fast! And it knows that being fast is linked to survival. There is no time to analyze or think rationally when we might be in danger, we just need to act! When it's time to make a fast decision, we not only can't rely on our rational brain, but we also need to shut it down.

As an illustration, let's see what happens when we meet someone for the first time. When two people initially encounter each other, the vast majority of their first impressions happen in a totally non-conscious way. That is, we connect and communicate with each other on myriad levels of which we are not consciously aware. That's because our two most primitive brains, reptilian and emotional, connect first. Because of this, our cognitive biases are instantly activated, thereby profoundly and immediately influencing how we perceive that other person.

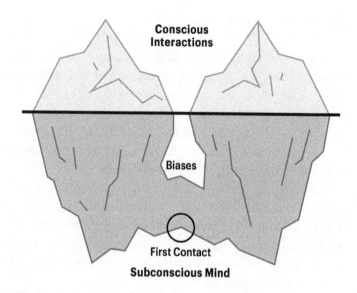

Do you know how long it takes our brain to decide if the person we just met is a friend or foe?

100 milliseconds!

System 1 ruled the roost over millions of years of human evolution, governing interactions in the prehistoric realm in the safest, smartest way. But is this protective stance conducive to excellent leadership in the present-day business environment? Not so much. Let's see why by continuing with this example of a first encounter between two people.

There are literally countless biases that could feed into any initial meeting, but resemblance is an easy place to start. Maybe I've had a negative experience with a person who looks similar to the one I'm meeting now. What are the consequences of that connection? My completely unconscious, instantly registered associations will feed a false first impression that will strongly influence my conscious interactions. There's a high probability that I will have a relatively negative reaction to whatever that person says or does, as compared with someone else who doesn't have the same similarity.

The opposite happens as well. If a person reminds me of someone I had a positive experience with, whatever our interaction might be, there is a high probability I will have a bias toward a positive perception of this person.

This associative phenomenon also occurs in new situations, instantly and profoundly coloring our perceptions of our environment/context with past associations.

Most people blindly believe in their first impressions and will follow them as if they represent an important truth. But the idea of first impressions as a reliable guide to character or context is a myth. In general, these feelings and perceptions are inherently and inevitably tinged with our biases.

People tend to believe that first impressions are fueled by intuition—yet another myth. But this chapter won't delve into what intuition is or where it comes from. For our purposes, it's enough to know that our first impressions are almost entirely a product of our biases. Therefore, with any new contact or situation, we need to be extremely mindful of how our biases influence us as we build our first impressions, as well as those that follow over time. This becomes all the more important when we encounter others while in a leadership role, in which our impressions can have lasting consequences that shape others' lives in ways big and small.

Now, of course, you'd probably like to use your considerable initiative and power to dispose of these pesky biases. After all, those qualities brought you where you are today, right? Impossible. The only concrete possibility for arriving at a perception of reality that approximates objectivity and rational thought is by being aware of how—and how much—our biases influence us. After all, our biases are activated in a split second, at a neural level where we have zero control. As we interact for a longer period of time, we increase the possibility of changing our first impression, and thereby gaining a more accurate idea of that particular person or situation.

You don't know what you don't know... until you've actively taken the time to recognize your automatically filled-in knowledge gaps, your assumptions, your erroneous beliefs—in short, your biases. And, by the way, they represent an ongoing process, occurring not just initially but to some extent in every moment of our lives—if we are not mindful and proactive. Our biases are always at the ready to offer a defensive, generally deluded and non-helpful, often discriminatory first reaction.

My new-person example paints a very simple picture of how biases work. Obviously, it's all a bit more complicated than just one person in the past reminding you of someone in the present. But where do all those earlier connections come from? Do our brains store everything we've ever seen or done? If not, which experiences are more likely to be stored in our brains? And given all these possible factors, how exactly do our biases build up in our subconscious mind?

While we are going to cover techniques for conquering bias, it's important to first clearly understand how biases develop, because they have an enormous impact on our lives. Take the ways we subconsciously perceive and characterize gender. Think about your childhood and your school years. Bring to mind a tiny fraction of your memories of the information you took in over those years about what a boy or girl should be. Whether through stories, movies, and advertisements, or via your interactions with your peers, parents, or other children and adults, you received an unfathomable, immeasurable amount of input about gender. How males and females "should" behave. What being a "real man" or a "real woman" means.

Guess what? Every single one of those ideas and interactions left a mark on your consciousness. All along, your mind was gathering every bit of that information and then creating internal stories and coming to conclusions, both of which were fundamentally shaped by your experiences. Were all those ideas about gender positive? Of course not! In general, they weren't even factual. All of the media, people, and interactions that contributed to your internal gender story were influenced by their culture, their prejudices, and more. And the way you perceived each and every piece of information? Shaped, in addition, by your own personality.

Moreover, we are not born as a blank slate. We bring a lot of information in our genes, from our immediate genetic ancestors but also from our very distant human and hominid ancestors and beyond. Thus, throughout our lives, we are simultaneously being bombarded by information coming from our environment and processing that information using our own unique set of personal *and* genetic capacities. Biased information indeed!

Hey, don't feel bad about this. There is literally no other way to be human. If we want to do better, our only option is to become more self-aware about our biases—and then learn how to deal with them to mitigate mistakes.

Defining Bias—and Assessing Its Scope

A more precise and comprehensive definition of cognitive biases can help us progress on this journey by giving us a better idea of what we are facing and how common the issue of bias truly is. Also known as unconscious inferences, biases are what Mahzarin R. Banaji and Anthony G. Greenwald, authors of *Blindspot: Hidden Biases of Good People*, call "mindbugs." In their book, these authors cite the definition used by MIT scientist Edward Adelson: biases are "ingrained habits of thought that lead to errors in how we perceive, remember, reason and make decisions."

Through their research, Banaji, for years a professor of social ethics at Harvard University, and Greenwald, a social psychologist and professor of psychology at the University of Washington, have developed the most accurate and powerful bias-analysis test that has ever been devised. I highly recommend doing a web search for their Implicit Association Test (IAT) and taking it to get a sense of your own biases, as thousands of others already have.

The main characteristic of this test is that it measures the speed of our responses to a series of words and pictures, capturing and analyzing our response time as a proxy for implicit bias. This test has the amazing capacity to activate System 1 and avoid any interference from System 2. Many, including those who are major researchers in the field of implicit bias, find the biases reflected in their scores to be both surprising and troubling.

Everybody knows that people do not always "speak their minds." Many of us also suspect that people quite often do not "know their minds" either. Understanding such divergences is important for those of us who want to work on our self-awareness. The IAT method demonstrates our conscious-unconscious divergences much more precisely and convincingly than has ever been possible with previous tools. It's a tremendous success, not only because of its high level of participation, but also because it has been a huge eye-opener for so many people.

By now we have defined bias, and gained some idea of why we have biases and how they work. But being aware of our biases doesn't mean we don't still act under their influence—constantly. This is especially true when it comes to gender and race. I know, many of us consider ourselves to be open-minded, enlightened, not the type of person who would have these sorts of biases. That's why the IAT is so effective. It pushes you to respond in a way that bypasses your rational thinking. The test is designed to dig directly into our unconscious minds, using subtle word associations and visuals. It even has a time limit, further spurring on those of us who, in addition to our purported lack of bias, also consider ourselves to be "achievement-oriented."

One of Banaji and Greenwald's most astonishing findings was that not only do white people hold biases toward African Americans, and men toward women (as we might, sadly, expect), but African Americans can also hold the same implicit biases toward African Americans, and women toward women. This means, among other things, that we are often biased against ourselves! Prejudices and biases are ingrained in cultures in ways far more complex than heretofore imagined. Here's one very obvious yet remarkably persistent and pervasive example of bias: why do we use the words "black" or "dark" to convey negative connotations in so many instances? We have deep, hard, long-term work to do if we want to understand and change the wrong associations festering inside us and degrading our cultures and environments.

How Do We See the World?

We have been talking at length about the subjectivity of our observations as related to the split-second decisions our brains make. I'd like to take a closer look at this topic from another angle in order to reveal the truth about how we each experience our environments in our own disparate ways. We tend to believe we share the same perceptions, that, say, when we both see a car, you can describe exactly the same characteristics I am observing. That what catches my attention is the same thing that catches your attention. Even colors, we assume, are perceived by all of us in the same way. Not so.

I am presenting very basic examples, but we can go to more complex issues, too. Take how we interpret different aspects of our businesses, such as how we discern the actions that we must take depending on how we see and understand the market. Even when we are working with what is apparently very objective data—the company's balance sheet or income statement, for example—and we might naturally assume everyone in the organization understands that data in the same way, we would be incorrect. Far from being negative or alarmist, what I am getting at can be a fascinating and generative aspect of life, and it's something we humans have known for millennia. As a well-known ancient saying explains, "We don't see the world as it is, we see the world as we are."

We all wear glasses with different lenses constructed by our own history, our own past experiences, our own ways of reacting to our environment. Our biases are activated over milliseconds, in tandem with a lifetime of external input and internal and epigenetic factors that shape our perceptions and reactions in ways that make each of us unimaginably distinct from others. Since we have no way of moving outside of this matrix, increasing our awareness of how we perceive and react will enable us to transform this apparent barrier into an added value.

That's where the neuroscience knowledge I've gained over the years comes in very handy. Sometimes an organization will hire me to enact my coaching process in order to address a difficult situation, whether with a boss, a peer, or a team. Because of our biases, applying the concept of empathy alone is often not enough. In general, people have a bias toward considering themselves highly empathetic by default, without knowing exactly what that really implies. Then, on top of that assumption, people's perceptions and actions are ruled by the many biases discussed in this chapter. My job is to help clients to see the perspective of the other person from their (that is, the client's) own reality. In other words, my technique doesn't involve talking about what happens to someone else or how that person feels, but instead I am enabling my client to actually experience how they themselves would feel in the other's shoes. In this way, we can mobilize our natural biases to work for us—and get ahead of those biases that don't.

I remember working with a top senior bank executive who was extremely critical of his boss. He could not understand what he defined as his boss's lack of attention to and affirmation of the hard work he himself put in day after day. Our sessions were filled with complaints about what his boss was or was not doing according to my client's biased notions of what was correct (among others, this involved *false consensus bias*, which I will delve into soon).

To inspire effective self-reflection, I tried "promoting" my client to a "super boss" role, and then prompting him to describe how he would lead his team from that position. It was a fascinating process to see how, over just a few sessions, he came to understand that if he were in his boss's shoes, he would be acting in exactly the same way. The key factor was broadening his viewpoint away from the limiting lens of his biases, and moving him toward the big picture, and to the level of pressure he would be seeing/feeling in his boss's place. In the end, my client was actually promoted to an even more senior position—and found that he was able to almost seamlessly understand his new roles and responsibilities, as well as those of his new team. After having diligently and successfully practiced self-awareness over time, his empathy popped, and he *got it*.

Maybe at this moment you're thinking that my message is "it's all about you." Well, most of the time, it is... sort of. But I would reframe this to clarify that "it's all about the components of your lens." We can only perceive and understand what the components of our lens allow us to see and comprehend. And let's be very clear. The components of our lens can change at any time; in fact, they are in a state of permanent revision and change. It's up to us to consciously decide how we want our lens to change, and in what direction.

Another client, a middle-level investment company executive, had high ambitions for her career but seemed stalled. She was living the phrase "what brought you here will not necessarily take you there." Up to that point, her attitude hadn't been considered aggressive. She'd been perceived as proactive, a bit pushy, determined, firm in her convictions: all very positive traits in the right context—and a big part of how she'd gotten where she was.

It was interesting to observe how the leaders in her company changed their perspective according to level. My client's pushy attitude had always been affirmed as a plus, along with the way she didn't easily accept others' opinions and always spoke first, without listening. Now, her personality— long considered an asset—was becoming a barrier. And when her bosses changed the rules and parameters about her attitude, it was very difficult for her to figure out what she should do.

Many biases were included in her perceptions along the way. For instance, *confirmation bias* (more on that soon) had been her guide through many decisions in which she tested her worth. At this new stage, her managers began asking her to work on her blind spots, by learning to listen, empowering others, developing people, and so on. Things no longer centered on her, as they previously had. It took a lot of coaching to help her implement a process of self-awareness around how her biases did not serve her anymore. Essentially, she had been relying on System 1 and had to learn how to give predominance to System 2 in order to advance. To get her where she needed to be, we worked on a self-reflective technique to explore and develop a healthier personality. I started by having her confront her old self from the perspective of her improved personality style. Guided metacognition, or "thinking about thinking," allowed her to see herself from the outside and analyze her own thoughts and actions, thereby leveraging her System 2 to grow more conscious of her no-longer-useful assumptions and tendencies. With these tools in place, my client was able to nurture new strengths and attitudes that didn't so often default to System 1 and her automatic biases.

Did that fix everything? Unfortunately, no. But my client wasn't the only one who had biases. One of the hardest barriers she faced was that, over time, her bosses had built up a negative *halo effect bias* toward her. By the time I worked with her, everything she did or said was deemed aggressive and counterproductive, rather than, as before, determined and productive. In addition, *gender bias* unquestionably played a part in the ways she was judged in the organization.

My client progressed very well in her own inner development, but it was not enough to have a positive effect on her bosses, and she had to leave the company. She ended up at another organization, where she was able to benefit from her own transformation as well as from the relative lack of halo effect and gender biases on the part of her new managers.

In both of these examples from my coaching practice, we can see how biases have far-reaching, often unrecognized, and/or negative implications for leadership when not addressed head-on. Let's pivot to some specific types of biases, some of which I've mentioned here, to get a better idea of what we are up against.

A Bias Sampler

How many biases do we have, typically?

Researchers Buster Benson and John Manoogian III created a codex of more than two hundred biases grouped into four major categories. Their findings do not necessarily mean that we have only two hundred biases, or even that each of us has these specific biases, but at least they give us a good idea of their extensive quantity and variety.

How often do our biases influence our lives? In a few words: all the time. In every conversation, when we drive, when we shop, when we go for a walk, when we choose, develop, and lead our teams... our mind will be influenced by our biases. They are everywhere!

As you've probably realized by now, we don't necessarily recognize our biases right away, if ever. We are so used to them that they seem to be a normal part of life, a standard, "correct" way of perceiving the world. And remember, what feels "right" to us activates the reward centers in our brains, effectively reinforcing biased perceptions and behaviors. So, we are initially going to have to work hard to counteract that formidable positive incentive. Over time, we need to show our brains that working against bias is ultimately the "correct," reward-worthy way to go.

Let's explore a select few types, in preparation for proactively addressing the manifestations of bias you'll eventually ferret out in your own brains. I would like to warn you, though: your five brains' first reaction when reading each of the following examples will be denial. It is not easy to accept that our daily lives are plagued with these mindbugs.

The following are just a few of the different cognitive biases that have a powerful influence on how we think, feel, and behave.

Confirmation Bias

Once I arrive at a conclusion, have an idea about a topic, or build a hypothesis, I will likely use, even select, the information I subsequently take in to confirm my assumption. This is because people tend to attach more weight to information that reinforces their previously held beliefs. Because of this, two people who have very different perspectives can hear the same story and each interpret that story in line with their disparate points of view.

In any business situation, we must make decisions that involve risk. Usually, we develop an idea about the most appropriate decision and then, when we discuss it with the rest of the team, our mind essentially looks for information that will confirm that decision. In fact, some managers judge their employees according to how much they help to confirm their previous ideas. Confirmation bias can impel us to make inferior decisions because we are liable to consider fewer key factors and/or ignore other opinions that may be more insightful, bold, or innovative.

Hindsight Bias

In my home country of Argentina, we have many sayings related to the bias referred to in the English-language saying "hindsight is 20/20." One of them is this: "On Mondays everyone becomes the best soccer coach in town." Soccer is our national sport, and, after the big weekend games, everyone discusses how things *should have gone* for their preferred team to win.

This common cognitive bias arises from our tendency to see events, even random ones, as more predictable and "known" than they are. Following exams, students often look back on the questions and think, "Of course! I knew that!"— even though they were unable to recall the answer during the test. Investors look back and believe that they could have predicted which tech companies would become dominant forces. But did they make those predictions at the time? Not necessarily!

A study on hindsight bias published in *Perspectives on Psychological Science* showed that our memories are not fixed— we change them all the time, especially when we receive new information about a past event. If someone's financial prediction regarding an investment was X, but then they come to know that the real result was Y, their memory will tell them that their original prediction was somewhere between X and Y. This means that hindsight bias may direct leaders away from learning vital lessons—or make them feel they already know more than they do.

Availability Heuristic Bias

This bias involves the tendency to estimate the probability of something happening based on how many examples readily come to mind. For example, it's very easy to recall plane crashes. And when we do so, our brains do not necessarily remember that flights are by far the safest mode of motorized transportation ever. The most representative example of the availability heuristic is arguably the lottery. The mathematical probability of winning the lottery is one in many, many millions, sometimes billions! Yet stories of lucky winners impel people to buy lottery tickets, again, and again, and again.

Naturally, savvy marketers rely on this bias to keep brands front of mind for consumers via ubiquitous advertising.

In business, this bias can have a significant negative impact on our decision-making, because (believe it or not) the arguments that carry the greatest weight in our reasoning are generally those that we have heard most recently. On the other hand, when we do an objective, statistical study of a given situation, we will usually be directed toward a very different conclusion. Thus, big data analysis is a terrific tool for mitigating this type of bias. The more information we have, the more likely we are to understand the current factors that should be taken into account, along with the future probability of a given event.

Availability heuristic bias is essentially a mental shortcut that evolved to save us time in risk determination. The problem with relying on this way of thinking is that it often leads to poor estimates and bad decisions.

False Consensus Bias

We also tend to overestimate how much other people agree with us or see things the same way we do, which results in a false consensus effect. Not only does this bias lead people to erroneously believe that others agree with them, it also sometimes drives people to value their own opinions too highly. This probably originates with the ways we may share similar opinions with those close to us, and then tend to extrapolate from there. The false consensus bias may help us feel comfortable in the world, but it also impedes transformation and innovation at the personal and organizational levels.

Halo Effect Bias

When people are good at some particular thing, or even good-looking, we often assume they have superior capabilities in other areas as well. Conversely, this can also go in a negative direction when we perceive someone as bad at some specific thing, or unattractive, and take cognitive leaps form there. In business, marketing, politics, and beyond, the halo effect bias can have serious real-world repercussions, since, as studies suggest, being seen as attractive and/or capable in some area makes people think you possess additional stereotypically positive attributes (such as intelligence, communication skills, talents, and so on) that may have nothing to do with your looks or expertise.

Here's a seemingly silly but true example: a workplace study done in 2004 revealed that every inch an employee is above average height may potentially be worth $789 more in income per year. Why? Height is an attribute that tends to confer a positive halo effect!

In the absence of self-reflection and intentional efforts to counter them, leaders can be impelled in both directions by halo effect biases, awarding undeserved responsibilities and honors to the tall, the good-looking, the skilled in some area, while holding others back based on the opposite attributes.

Is this how you want to run your business?

Gender Bias

Many of the previous types of biases play into one form of very common discrimination and stereotyping that I alluded in my discussion of the client who was having trouble with the way her bosses perceived her. It's well known that people judge the same personality traits differently depending on whether they are expressed by a man or a woman. An article in the *Harvard Business Review* analyzed gender biases in two hundred performance review processes. The authors found that these interactions were rife with double standards. Another analysis in *Forbes* described how a go-getting, assertive personality will typically be defined as positive in a man and aggressive in a woman. Or a woman might be described as "edgy" while a man might be called "rough around the edges." The latter is a temporary, fixable state; the former is deemed a character flaw—even though we are really talking about the same behavior in both cases.

We Can Challenge Our Biases

Now that you've learned the basics of a few very common biases, I'm confident you can see how important self-awareness is in this area. Each of these biases can blur the lens through which we see and react to the world. Leaders who master this facet of their personalities become at once wiser and more efficient, steadier and more open to growth.

Helping people deal with their unconscious inferences or biases, their mindbugs, makes up a huge part of my daily work. As the world has become more "woke" in general, leaders especially are being called to task for the roles they have played—and continue to play—in perpetuating bias. At the same time, those self-same leaders have amazing and extensive opportunities to spearhead major organizational and societal transformations!

When I challenge my clients by offering and eliciting different perspectives, they're able to reframe situations with the benefit of new wisdom and increased internal and external agility. I constantly defy the objectivity of their perceptions to help them become aware of their biases; the richness of the results they achieve justifies this approach again and again.

Likewise, if you want to get ahead of these omnipresent biases, you have to be ready to do the same for yourself and your team. Only then will you begin to foster clarity in your perceptions and reactions, moving from automatic reliance on System 1 to mindful implementation of System 2, and generating a clear lens through which you'll improve your decision-making, flexibility, and many other aspects of your leadership.

The work that I do as an executive coach is integrally grounded in building communication bridges between different parts of ourselves and between ourselves and others. You can master this process on your own if you have the right information and are willing to put key insights into action. Both types of connections can benefit from doing the hard work of incisive self-analysis suggested in this chapter, along with practicing the techniques I'll explore in the next. While our biases are inevitably entrenched in our brains, we can be proactive and curious about them rather than evasive or judgmental. We can embed other elements to mitigate their effects, and take brain-smart approaches to spur evolution.

I'm guessing you're ready to take action to hone your decision-making and other vital leadership skills that may be diminished by bias—and can also be vastly improved by skillfully counteracting your brains' instinctive responses. Read on for an in-depth look at the real-life impacts of biases in the workplace, followed by practical, actionable ideas managers can start implementing right away, and continue to grow from over the longer term.

Mitigating Biases for Better Decisions, Relationships, and Results

EADY TO tackle your biases and become a wiser, more successful leader and human being? Well, we've got work to do. As Nobel laureate Richard Feynman used to say, "The first principle is that you must not fool yourself—and you are the easiest person to fool." It's not that we intentionally deceive ourselves all the time so much as we construct stories that are consistent or aligned with our way of seeing life. In that process, we create less-than-ideal (in the bigger picture) situations and convince ourselves of things that are not exactly correct.

The best example of this phenomenon is what is called the Dunning–Kruger effect. This is a feeling of illusory superiority, seen when people with low competence in a given task vastly overestimate their performance. In general, it's not easy to recognize our own incompetence, and this leads to erroneous perceptions in the way we self-assess in various situations.

And guess what? Almost all of us are naturally incompetent when it comes to the task of identifying our own biases—as we saw when we took the quiz in the previous chapter!

But the thing is, our biases have immensely far-reaching implications for ourselves and for others, especially in the workplace. So, we *must* do better. In Chapter 8, we focused on understanding that we have biases, learned how they are formed and become entrenched, and recognized why they are so instantaneous as to be largely inevitable. In this chapter, we will do the very worthwhile work of delving more deeply into the destructive impacts of biases and then developing constructive techniques to counteract these insidious mind-bugs. We will learn to create space for better communication, healthier teams, and stronger, more productive connections, thereby generating increased inclusion, boosting innovation, and improving our decision-making and listening skills—to name just a few benefits—along the way.

The Consequences of Bias

Let's analyze the damaging effects of our biases, focusing on the working world. Honestly, the list could be endless! But let's stick to the typical biases that interfere in common workplace situations.

Job interviews are a great place to start because they are positively *loaded* with biases. Nowadays, companies are determined to find ways to conduct interviews that are as free of biases as possible. To date, this goal has only very, very rarely been achieved. The most common biases in this context have to do with race, gender, nationality, ethnicity or local (neighborhood, city, state) origin, education, and behavior, as well as those related to comparisons between the interviewer and interviewee.

The following list is not comprehensive. As you will probably suspect as you read through them, similar biases are also likely to occur in other corporate contexts—from how we interact in meetings to general office dynamics, formal performance reviews to casual (but potentially productive) conversations, client relations to employee promotions.

Primacy of First-Impression Bias

As discussed in Chapter 8, this complex bias subconsciously shapes our reactions to a new person within milliseconds. The downside? Whatever our primary impression was will influence every subsequent decision we make about that individual! Furthermore, our rational brain will always find ways to justify whatever messages we receive from that momentary subconscious assessment. This bias plays a decisive role in interviews. Even when an interviewer is aware of it, they cannot avoid judging absolutely everything about the interviewee—physical appearance, how they walk, talk, sit—from moment one. Thus, interviewers must be highly trained to avoid being ruled by System 1; instead, they must be professionals in using System 2 to override and circumvent it. How do we get there? Steady System 2 intervention requires a high level of self-awareness, coupled with practice, practice, practice—basically, keeping it front of mind until it becomes a habit.

Similar-to-Me Bias

This mindbug seeks out interests, skills, and background elements that match with the interviewer, unconsciously looking for similarities. Any such commonality will have a positive effect on us, making us feel good because those similar aspects are familiar—and therefore "safe." Simply put, we tend to like people who are like us. The reverse is also true.

Either way, this bias strongly influences interviewers' decisions regarding candidates. In addition to making interviews tricky, this bias can make the workplace less inclusive, less diverse, less creative, less equitable, less objective, and, in the end, less productive. Interviewers looking to transcend this bias must devise rational ways to tread a careful line between finding candidates who to some extent feel "comfortable" and will integrate well into the team as is, but will also, more importantly, expand the team's qualities and capacities. The secret here is to learn how to feel at ease with discomfort (which is actually quite often an indicator of progress). In addition, we must define very clear objectives from the beginning: *Do we need diversity on our team?* That clarity of purpose will prepare our "lens" to identify diversity as an added value.

Confirmation Bias

Our tendency to interpret, favor, and recall information in a way that supports our prior beliefs definitely complicates the interviewing process. Interviewers listen through a filter that amplifies comments or opinions that resonate with our own ideas. We unconsciously seek replies that match our own established thoughts and perceptions. This turns interviews into an exam in which only we know the correct answers to our questions. Each matching response is a positive mark for the candidate. Think about it: Do those "correct" replies indicate anything about the candidate's suitability for the position? Or do they confirm the interviewer's assumptions? Simply asking yourself these questions is a good place to start countering this bias.

Gender Bias

Among other impacts, this pervasive bias leads us to direct our attention differently in interviews depending on the candidate's gender. We tend to observe and highlight aspects of women's attitudes and personalities, and focus on men's professional achievements. Hence, for this and other biased reasons, we tend to deem men more qualified than women. Here is just one example of a serious bias with an amazing solution. Historically, the proportion of female musicians in symphony orchestras was very, very low (typically 5 percent or less). When orchestras began installing screens during auditions so judges could only hear and not see performers, the chance that a female musician would make it past the first round increased by 50 percent. Awareness of implicit bias is the sine qua non tool for mitigating this age-old bias, but we also need to actively cultivate workarounds for when we (incorrectly) think we are actually being objective. Our reptilian brain can be remarkably tricky that way... and we need to find ways to turn the tables!

How Bias Shows Itself in Our Working Lives

When we see through a biased lens, we are unable to genuinely listen and connect, never mind see an individual for all their unique attributes and capabilities. Clearly, these biases can lead us to choose the wrong candidate, thereby impacting our team and our performance for years to come. I've already suggested some initial ideas for decreasing bias in earlier sections in this chapter. However, before I offer more tools, I want to explore some additional ways bias plays a negative role in our working lives, in order to spark motivation and inspire you to dedicate yourself to the cause of fighting bias in yourself and others.

As with the interview process, our approach to dealing with customers is rife with biases. These days, we talk a lot about empathizing with our clients, but are we oriented by real empathy or by our cognitive biases? Sure, looking for common themes to nurture closer relationships is a good technique for winning clients, but what happens to those who are quite different from us? Are we going to do business only with people who look and behave like us? It doesn't make a lot of sense, does it? And yet if you look at the way high-level business was conducted not so long ago, you'd see almost 100 percent white men who went to certain schools, wouldn't you? And now? Only *mostly* white men who went to certain schools.

Let's say you're negotiating with a diverse group of people representing a desired potential client. Based on just the limited list detailed in the previous section, you're likely to focus on and feel most comfortable with and drawn to the person in that group who:

- Makes a "good" first impression based on a lifetime of biases

- Is most like you

- Seems to share your beliefs

- And, probably, *seems* to have the most impressive accomplishments (e.g., is male) or to appear more charming and attractive (in the case of a woman)

Yet one of the most frequent recommendations in sales training is to avoid making any assumptions about who may have the purchasing decision. Don't even try! Guessing leads to error in the majority of cases. Why? Because your impressions are flooded with your biases. And when you direct your efforts erroneously, you're more likely to miss out on key connections, and, hence, the sale.

The most successful negotiators and salespeople are those with a high AQ, or adaptability quotient. These individuals are able to avoid some of these pitfalls by being flexible, open-minded, resilient, and able to unlearn. Yes, I do mean *unlearn*, that is, they have the capacity and disposition to replace old knowledge with new, better information. Such people are able to establish productive relationships by connecting more authentically with others as human beings, not as representations of stereotypes or other unconscious learned/ingrained biases.

We can all grow our AQ. Self-awareness around both our biases and the characteristics of our personality are key to this evolution. Here again, we see the vital importance of addressing our biases for the greater good of the enterprise, not to mention personal advancement. As Daniel Kahneman warns, "The vast majority of human decisions are based on biases, beliefs, and intuition, not facts or logic." It's time for leaders to take the initiative in eradicating these unfair, anti-productive barriers in the workplace.

Promoting Diversity and Inclusion

This chapter cannot possibly cover the immense and sensitive topics of diversity and inclusion. But we absolutely must acknowledge—and take a hard look at—the deep, entrenched, and long-standing connections between a *lack* of diversity/inclusion and bias.

Let's begin by revisiting the amygdala's influence on our brains as related to our current topic. As we have discussed previously, our two amygdalae are programmed to process any physical or behavioral differences or changes as potentially dangerous. Remember that the amygdala functions like a radar system, and that its main mission is to constantly check if anything around us poses a potential threat. The moment it detects a person who looks or acts differently from us or the people we're used to, the amygdala puts the reptilian brain on alert, signaling that a potential danger is nearby. The reptilian brain then gets us prepared to attack, freeze, or escape, as the situation allows.

What can we do to overcome this primitive reaction? We can find ways to regain control through our rational brain. And the only way we can overcome the influence of our biases on our reactions and behaviors and neutralize the enormous power of this instinctive, outdated reaction is by activating System 2.

Before we get to the how-to part, let's make something very clear: diversity and inclusion are not analogous. In the words of Vernā Myers, a powerful activist, diversity training educator, and strategist for justice: "Diversity is being invited to the party. Inclusion is being asked to dance." And even diversity and inclusion alone do not make for a perfect world. To bring in another apt quote, this one from authors Liz Fosslien and Mollie West Duffy:

> Accessibility is being able to get in the building,
> Diversity is getting invited to the table,
> Inclusion is having a voice at the table,
> Belonging is having your voice heard at the table.

Yet the work we do to put System 2 in charge will lead to progress on all of these vital fronts. I am convinced that the most important work toward inclusion, diversity, accessibility, and belonging happens simply through getting to know each other better. The more the amygdala comes in contact with what is different, the less it will react. When what was different becomes the norm, it is no longer subconsciously perceived as dangerous. However, even to get to this point of basic interaction, human to human, we must strive mightily to overcome our biases!

Without a doubt, the internet is one of the most powerful and effective instruments toward this objective—as long as it is used with that intent. Recent generations are not subject to the same concrete physical barriers to contact that past generations faced. For the first time in history, we have the sensory experience of being interconnected worldwide, which makes for one of our most powerful tools for increasing diversity and inclusion. Despite our physical distance, 2020 was an unprecedented year in which this global social closeness could be felt more intensely than ever before. We had no choice.

After living and working in Prague—the relatively diverse geographical center of Europe and the headquarters of many large multinational companies—I went to live and work in Toronto, Canada, which the United Nations calls the most diverse city in the world. In this bastion of multiculturalism, over half of the residents were born outside of Canada. In these cities, I was exposed to a remarkably high level of diversity both at work and in my social life, which helped me understand the differences between diversity and real inclusion.

You see, even as we outwardly enact pro-diversity policies, biases continue to rear their ugly heads. Two challenges arise as an almost inevitable consequence of diversity. On the one hand, we encounter and express privilege and, on the other, we deal with our own and others' microaggressions and microaffirmations.

Let's start with privilege, widely defined as "a benefit enjoyed by an individual or group beyond what is available to others." Privileges are impossible to avoid, and they change all the time, depending on circumstances, location, social context, and many other parameters.

And privilege doesn't just pose problems because of inequality and discrimination. Here's another way to frame privilege, from narrative designer and writer David Gaider, indicating how privilege also leads to stagnation and inertia: "Privilege is when you think something is not a problem because it's not a problem for you personally."

Ever hear any white people say racism doesn't exist anymore? Privilege.

Guess what? From the moment there is diversity, there are privileges, which are in essence generated as a function of that often cherished and sought-after diversity.

So... what can we do? Activate System 2! Are you aware of your privileges? How about those you lack? Don't just go with your knee-jerk responses—instead, take the time to allow your rational brain to predominate (we will explore straightforward, pragmatic ways to do so soon, in this chapter's tools). In the same way that it's impossible to eliminate biases, we cannot eliminate privileges. We can work with all our hearts and minds toward equal rights and possibilities for everyone, but we cannot change the structure of our System 1 brains to stop them from registering and reacting in biased ways to diversity.

Nonetheless, we can start to compensate in the opposite direction by actively recognizing and proactively accepting differences; moreover, we can develop our awareness of our privileges. How, exactly, our experience of life—within one culture or another, within one physical aspect or another, within one gender or another—impacts us is 100 percent personal. It's the result of a complex, intricate, entirely unique combination of our genetic information, our environments (including the people around us) over our lifetimes, and the intersections of these factors.

Our experiences thus affect our lives in ways that those who are not having the same current experience inflected by the same lifetime of precise genetics and environments may find impossible to understand. This is the main reason why judging others' reactions to diversity, inclusion, privilege, or the lacks thereof is not only not very compassionate—it's also pure nonsense.

In the same way, it's not easy to be aware of our privileges—or the benefits they bestow. What is natural or "normal" for us is not natural or "normal" for everyone. What feels to us like harmless, insignificant self-expression or perhaps a mild joke may for others represent a deep offense or a direct, if "subtle," way to highlight difference in a negative way.

Privilege manifests constantly in the workplace. It determines the trajectory of our professional lives, influencing our career development, the ways we can succeed in our businesses, how a team can be productive—or cause professional damage for some or all of its members.

Microaggressions and microaffirmations play a huge role in this process.

Microaggressions can be defined as those acts (including spoken and written words, images, and more), generally carried out by someone possessing privileged status, that stereotype or denigrate the recipients. Arising from racial, gender, ethnic, sexual, aesthetic, religious, and other biases, they are typically subtle and indirect—thereby often allowing the perpetrator to excuse, justify, and/or rationalize their biased, privileged, harmful behavior.

Here are some common statements that inflict microaggressions:

- "I went to see a woman doctor."

- "It's great you don't have any accent." (When said to someone who is assumed to come from another country because of their race, appearance—including style of dress—ethnicity, and so on.)

- "You are doing such a great job." (When said to a disabled employee who is not doing any better than anyone else.)

- "You don't sound Black."

- "I'm immune to racism because I have friends of color."

- "I never would have guessed you were gay."

See how each comment *seems* to be "complimentary" and well meaning... but *isn't actually so*? I'm sure you can recall similar remarks that may have affected you or others around you. Because such statements are so common, so embedded in our cultures, they can be hard to recognize.

Here's an example from my own time as a workshop leader in Canada. As both an icebreaker and a true statement, I would always start with the same phrase: "Let me know when my Spanglish is not clear enough; I love to learn." Almost invariably, someone would say, "Your English is much better than my Spanish." Typically, however, the person saying this didn't speak a word of Spanish. And, yes, in general they were also trying to be nice. But the truth is, that response represents a microaggression. Do you see why?

So what can we do about these generally well-meaning yet, in actual effect, aggressive words and actions? When properly deployed, microaffirmations can actually work as an antidote to microaggressions. MIT ombudsman Mary Rowe defines microaffirmations as "tiny acts of opening doors to opportunity, gestures of inclusion and caring, and graceful acts of listening."

Microaffirmations include:

- Giving the benefit of the doubt

- Appropriately affirming the work of others

- Providing clear expectations for performance and explicit acknowledgment of associated accomplishments

- Asking others for their opinions

- Offering comfort and support in stressful situations

- Using friendly facial expressions and gestures

Leaders may also want to use imagery and storytelling that serve to counter stereotypes as another form of affirmation in the workplace. Formal or informal, institutional or personal, any small act of kindness or decency, sensitively offered, can function as a microaffirmation.

So, as leaders, what can we learn from all this? Believe it or not, if you've truly been taking in this information on the impacts of biases, you're already well on your way toward enacting System 2. If you are able to accept that we are not necessarily aware which of our messages may contain micro-aggressions; if you can understand that we must ask more questions, more frequently, in order to learn and give room to others; if you can open your mind to offer collaboration and support, knowing that you may not see the full picture ... you are beginning to lead with System 2.

In an article on bosses and biases published in the *Harvard Business Review*, Joan Williams and Sky Mihaylo write: "You can't be a great manager without becoming a bias inter-rupter." Do you now know this to be true?

Mitigating Unconscious Cognitive Biases

We need to close the gap between our ideals and intentions and our actual behaviors and actions. Yes, that includes those of us who—despite ample evidence to the contrary—still think we are bias-free! I myself, an avowed non-racist, once asked an extremely tolerant, good-humored Black man in my audience the name of a Black actor in a movie. My biased question took mere seconds to emerge from my mouth and was immediately followed—too late to prevent my words—by deep shock, shame, and recognition. He was kind enough to respond, with a laugh, "Just because I'm Black doesn't mean I know the name of every single other Black person." So, I *personally* invite you to experiment with the ideas and exercises you'll find here, even if you'd put yourself in the (nonexistent) category of unbiased people.

Frankly, the world we live in can be *volatile, uncertain, complex, ambiguous*—so much so, in fact, that there is even a well-known acronym for it: VUCA. It's been all the more so during the pandemic, and we can certainly expect things to continue to be challenging after it ends. The most important facet of our VUCA context is that default solutions don't work anymore. We need to be creative, vigorously seeking to transform outdated practices and viewpoints, both of which have bias written all over them. In this quantum leap evolutionary shift, collaboration should be the name of the game. Indeed, it's the only way to move forward. In this process, we will need real diversity—of ideas, perceptions, backgrounds—if we truly hope to approach potential solutions from vital new perspectives.

Having seen just a few of the countless consequences of the presence of biases in the workplace, we can deduce that mitigating these damaging mindbugs might involve taking actions that entail positive consequences. Our decision-making processes are a great place to start! When we aggressively but wisely tackle the mindbugs that cloud our thought processes and impact our actions for the worse, we clear the way for increased clarity and positivity in our choices.

First and foremost, we need to create an authentic, concrete, enduring perception of being in an emotionally safe environment at work, without the fear of being discriminated against—both for ourselves and for our teams. We can take practical steps to ensure that everyone feels heard, and able to share without holding themselves back. These steps will lead to greater commitment, which directly translates into improved morale, flexibility, productivity, and results.

There is already plenty of information available on counteracting biases. I want to give you several tools that build further on the specialized knowledge base you've already been establishing throughout the previous chapters. Many of the exercises in this chapter resonate with prior practices, such as the work we did to create space in the day for our brains to rest and rejuvenate, or our efforts to cultivate serenity in the face of change.

I myself have seen how helpful these anti-bias tools are for leaders, and I'm confident they'll be extremely useful for you. We are going to tackle two areas of bias mitigation: things we ourselves can do, and harnessing group intelligence. I will also introduce a six-step plan that will allow you and your organization to actively work toward the goal of counteracting bias to forge stronger, more generative connections.

Working on Ourselves

Metacognition, the ability to observe oneself from outside, is the key to developing awareness and understanding of our own thought processes. This higher-order thinking skill stems from our rational brain, that is, System 2. While our primitive brains (System 1) will always exert some influence, we can actively improve our self-awareness and discernment, steering our brains toward rational control and less-biased, more positive and productive decisions, interactions, and so on. The following practices are designed to help you do so.

Tool: Exercises to Activate System 2

Use these approaches to disrupt your own biased thoughts and reactions. Try all of them (especially those that make you uncomfortable!), as often as possible, to clarify your lens. You can write them out, speak them aloud, or just think them through, but do your very best to be brutally honest. After all, you're talking to yourself!

Shine a flashlight on yourself. Don't automatically take your first responses or reactions to be correct. Those are your default responses, fed by System 1, that is, your biases. Don't forget, making that instinctive choice will not only seem like the "right" way to go, it will always make you *feel good*. It typically appears familiar: "This is me!" Nope, that's your biases bossing you around. Help System 2 lead by taking your time to consider all options as you approach any decision. In this context, even a minute or two can make all the difference.

Justify your decisions. Force yourself to come up with additional explanations for your own decisions. Practice explaining your choices to somebody else: How will you justify them? How can you convince a third party that your decisions are excellent ones? System 1 doesn't care about any of this—it's too busy being quick and vigilant. System 2 gets activated when you try to clear things up for "somebody else."

Practice constructive uncertainty. As we know very well by now, uncertainty is profoundly challenging for our brains. Its quickest and most direct effect is the activation of System 1. We must train ourselves to keep System 2 in control when we encounter uncertainty in situations and decisions. One of the best ways to do this is simply to pause, step back from, and observe our automatic thoughts whenever we are faced with something unexpected or novel. In this pause, take a few deep breaths, to soothe your five brains. This practice strengthens System 2, much as lifting weights strengthens your muscles. Another mode of constructive uncertainty entails actively placing yourself in new situations and exposing yourself to unfamiliar things, then using that same pause to learn and train yourself to become less reactive.

Challenge your first impressions. As with the previous exercise, first impressions arise almost entirely from System 1, that is, from our biases; likewise, new habits involving time and metacognition are the answer. It might sound simplistic to exercise System 2 from the get-go by observing but not buying into your immediate reactions, but it's actually an evolutionary leap of sorts. For millennia, humans have been succumbing to biased, outdated, limited impulses from our primitive brains. It's time to honor our second impressions, which do not come from a place of fear!

Explore awkwardness and discomfort. Remember, every single bit of information coming from System 1 has a pleasant impact on us. It's familiar, comfortable, "safe"/"protective," and easy to accept, *even if it involves fear and biases.* Why question it, then? Well, the comfort zone is almost entirely System 1 territory. Remember the perils of staying in the comfort zone (like those we discussed in Chapter 4)? Many vital, transformative aspects of twenty-first-century business excellence—groundbreaking ideas, truly agile approaches, and innovative solutions—elicit discomfort or awkwardness at first. They are inherently unfamiliar and, hence, uncomfortable. We must reprogram ourselves to remember that whatever feels familiar is not necessarily the best action to take.

Again, watch yourself: catch your gut reactions when it comes to change... and transcend them by opening up to these uneasy feelings that are merely indicators that something fresh and creative is happening.

Examine the opposite of every decision. This exercise is a very productive one. It is a way of calling on System 2, and therefore expanding our understanding. If you plan to say no, what might it mean to say yes? If you've decided to expect your team to embrace a hybrid work model or return to the office full time once they are vaccinated, what might it mean to encourage them to WFH indefinitely? When we practice investigating wildly different choices (perhaps especially the improbable or impossible ones) systematically and consistently, we dramatically increase our opportunities to incorporate different perspectives—and thus have a much higher chance of making better decisions.

Working with Our Teams

This is about teamwork, but a more fitting name is "collective intelligence." I don't think Thomas Malone—the Patrick J. McGovern Professor of Management at the MIT Sloan School of Management and the founding director of the university's Center for Collective Intelligence—explicitly connected his work on collective intelligence with biases, but I've found that his insights serve as an invaluable catalyst for mitigating bias in group settings. Malone defines collective intelligence as the "single statistical factor for a group that predicts how well the group will perform on a wide range of very different tasks."

In Chapter 8, we discussed the perils of solving problems through consensus while avoiding confrontation. What I'm talking about here is creating a space in which varied viewpoints are welcome, and disagreements are framed as productive, rather than as obstacles to the goal of total agreement. We must *almost invariably* disagree, at least initially, if we are to become more self-aware, more conscious of how we impact others—and if we want to come up with new ideas and learn new things!

As we already know, others can recognize our blind spots far more easily than we ourselves can. We are not separate entities but inextricably connected beings, and we can help each other enormously, especially in this particular issue. The most productive way to work on mitigating biases is through collective efforts. We cannot be anywhere near as effective by ourselves. Remember that we do not see the world as it is but as we are. We must learn to ask for help in order to enlarge our perceptions and be more conscious of our own biases.

Fortify your team with the following practices, and get ready to transcend heretofore insurmountable barriers to transformation (i.e., your—and their—biases).

Tool: Fostering Collective Intelligence

Your team relies on you to set the tone and convey what's acceptable and expected in the workplace, while also enabling each individual to shine, grow, and be heard. Handling these integral aspects of management wisely will nurture your collective intelligence for amazingly improved collaboration, inclusion, agility, and more. Here are several ways to reduce workplace bias while simultaneously improving your leadership and enhancing team dynamics. You'll find that in some ways these mirror the individual practices above, insofar as they represent group-level means for triggering System 2.

Empower everyone to call out biases. Let your people know that we fundamentally need others to point out where we could be doing better, so we can all grow—together.

Well-constituted teams that feel psychologically safe as a group can interact to mitigate biases. One individual's insight into another's (or a subgroup's) bias can be life-changing for both parties, as well as for the team as a whole. The key is agreeing on what to do about this type of observation, when to do it, how to communicate about it, and with whom. Clear procedures will minimize negativity and maximize potential evolution for all concerned.

Make decisions collectively. No, I don't mean you should insist on reaching consensus for every decision (whew!). This approach is more about being open to different perspectives on the issue at hand before deciding how to act. Making decisions collectively means listening to every single opinion, giving room for debate and dissent. Those additional perspectives give you and your team a better chance of coming to the best possible decision.

Ask for feedback. Do not wait passively to receive feedback; periodically request input about your performance. In my work, when the objective of the coaching mandate is to help my client broaden their self-awareness regarding the impact of their actions, I always recommend appointing a trusted, respected colleague as a "controller" with whom to check in periodically (for instance, after each team meeting). Taking in feedback without reacting defensively helps to reprogram your brains, especially by activating System 2. Without outside input, it's almost impossible to avoid making decisions under the influence of our blind spots. Hearing from others can allow us to draw a new neurological map of our behavior; only then are we prepared to walk in the right direction. Once my clients understand the value of this process, and see how much it enhances their decision-making, asking for feedback becomes an imperative facet of their leadership.

Try to create multiple opportunities for feedback throughout your team, so that everyone can benefit from constructive input. As above, ensuring clarity in your guidelines for providing feedback will temper reactivity and generate healthier interactions.

Overcoming Biases in Companies

We have talked about how to mitigate biases by working on ourselves and by leveraging collective intelligence. Now, we will discuss how companies can work to fight unconscious cognitive bias from within the organization itself. The six-step program that I am about to outline is designed to deploy a pragmatic, science-backed approach to help guide organizations through this process.

Tool: Six Steps to Overcoming Biases in Organizations

Companies looking to mitigate bias need actionable, real-life solutions to this pervasive challenge. Whether you are in the C-suite or at another managerial level, you'll find much to work with here, especially since most of these steps can be implemented to counteract biases at both the team and corporate levels. Given all the reasons detailed in this and the previous chapter, you know that investing in building genuine inclusion and creating a safe space that celebrates all perspectives and opinions isn't just the "right" thing to do—it's good business.

STEP 1: **Use surveys, focus groups, facilitated discussions, or other methods/data to identify the most common biases in your company.** Every organization has its own biases, and every employee has their own unique experience within that bias matrix. The basic concepts I've shared in this and the previous chapter apply to all contexts, as does the explanation of how they work. Nevertheless, the particular prevailing biases of each organization merit a closer look. They will only be revealed through sensitive data collection (whether quantitative and/or qualitative), and can only be effectively addressed if brought out into the open.

As an example of how to go about this, I'll share an experience I had while coaching the leadership team of a high-tech company. We were working very intensively on unconscious cognitive biases, among other topics. In that company, ethnic diversity was the most celebrated hallmark. As well, the proportion of women and men was roughly equal. Therefore, the most commonly known biases were quite well managed. When I started working with leadership on this issue, it was not easy for them to identify which biases might indeed characterize their company. It took them a while, but finally we made some progress. Several biases were identified, but the one they all agreed on was level of education. The majority of employees at this company had doctorates! Among these highly educated people, the predominant bias was to judge others according to the level of education achieved. They found it difficult to listen to the opinions of people who hadn't earned their respect based on educational attainment.

This may sound logical, but it isn't. Advanced degrees and institutional prestige do not necessarily correlate with common sense, or excellent strategic or analytical thinking. These leaders faced numerous complex challenges, and they needed different perspectives—all the time—to come up with great solutions. While many people in the organization were perfectly capable of providing a range of much-needed perspectives, they were not necessarily heard by leadership if their academic background was not deemed adequate by the managers' biased standards. Bringing this bias into the open helped to counter it—and helped the organization, too.

STEP 2: Look for connectors who can advocate as diversity and inclusion champions in the organization. In 1994, students at Pennsylvania's Albright College invented the game "Six Degrees of Kevin Bacon," in which the challenge was to connect every film actor to Bacon in six cast lists or fewer. Now often called "Bacon's law," the six-degrees of separation theory has been affirmed many times through various research projects. One of the most interesting efforts came from Microsoft. They studied records of 30 billion electronic conversations among 180 million people in various countries and concluded that indeed we can usually be linked by tracing, on average, six or fewer connections.

All of this research relates to the science of networking. Ultimately, what these studies actually showed was not that we are all connected to everyone on earth. Instead, they revealed that some people are more connected than others, and that many of those traced connections go through those same highly connected individuals to reach lots of others. These human hubs or connectors (also discussed at length in Chapter 5, regarding their role in change processes) represent a vital, constitutive factor in human networks.

In every organization, there are certain individuals who are connected with many more people than most others in the organization. They know about everything and everyone and, in turn, transmit and distribute all kinds of information. In general, these connectors or hubs tend to have particularly good relationships with their co-workers (and others). They're credible, and people listen to them. What better way to use these natural channels for spreading information than to work with them to counter bias? These connectors will accelerate and multiply the impact of the anti-bias ideas and tactics that you want to distribute in the organization.

STEP 3: Enact choice architecture (or nudging) to permeate the company with reminders that will help people make better choices. Richard Thaler, winner of the 2017 Nobel Memorial Prize in Economic Sciences for his contributions to behavioral economics, co-authored a very successful, influential book called *Nudge: Improving Decisions about Health, Wealth, and Happiness* (with Cass R. Sunstein). Their model proposes using "choice architecture"—that is, positive reinforcement and indirect suggestions, or "nudges"—as effective ways to shape the behavior and decision-making of groups and individuals. Many countries nowadays have a department of choice architecture that's tasked with using nudges to support goals such as getting community members to pay their taxes on time.

Nudges are demonstrably more effective than notifications. While notifications become less impactful the more often they are sent, nudges are the opposite: employees turn to them more and more over time. In fact, one app that specializes in delivering these "nudges" has found that engagement rates can reach as high as 95 percent.

What's the difference? While notifications are informative, generic alerts, nudges are more personal, actionable. They usually also offer a clear solution, while nonetheless leaving the actual decision in the receiver's power.

With a decent understanding of how people think, it's possible to use sensible, sensitive "choice architecture" to nudge them toward making the best decisions for themselves, their families, and their society—all without restricting their autonomy and personal choice. Furthermore, a Swedish study found that, in general, nudges help people build better work habits, get more done in less time, and connect more closely and genuinely with their colleagues. So why not leverage the power of nudges to mitigate biases in organizations?

It's best to adapt your chosen nudges to the characteristics and culture of your organization, as well as to its unique prevailing biases. Here are a few bias-related questions and ideas to get you started:

- "How much do you know about your colleagues' cultures?"
- "Who did you ask for feedback today?"
- "If you are not actively including, you are probably accidentally excluding."
- "Diversity = Different Perspectives = Better Results."

STEP 4: Create inclusion contests. We can leverage the power of competition in a positive way by initiating organization-wide activities around fighting bias. When we add an element of originality and fun to the mix, by using contests and prizes to solicit anti-bias ideas and proposals, we are signaling the importance of this effort while inherently building bridges for participation. In addition to generating company-specific approaches to bias, this step will give employees the opportunity to present their ideas to the entire organization, whether via publishing them in the company's newsletter or as a blog on the company's website, enacting them as policies or activities, or any other form of recognition/reward.

STEP 5: Implement bias-busting educational programs. The better we know each other, the higher the probability we'll get along. The more I learn about my colleagues in general—their cultures, habits, hobbies, families, dreams—the more I will be able to find areas with which to identify and empathize. What really happens in our brains is that the more information I have about those around me, the less likely they are to activate my amygdala's negative responses, thereby decreasing the chances of triggering my survival reaction. Basically, as we get familiar with each other, we actually start to sidestep biased reactions at the neural level!

Company-wide (or team-wide) campaigns can promote this process. When you implement programs that encourage and aid employees to know more about their fellow employees' cultures and how they might add value to the organization, you're facilitating very real and beneficial brain shifts for all concerned.

Remember that everything we perceive as different can awaken a self-protective, biased reaction. Whether we actually fight, freeze, or flee, or simply experience an internal reaction, this limits openness, listening skills, and so on.

The objective of such educational campaigns is thus twofold: first, familiarizing employees with one another to organically reduce bias; and, second (a related endeavor that we covered in more detail in Chapter 5), shifting the paradigm from "everything different can be dangerous" to "everything different can bring value, help us grow, add new possibilities to our work, and drive better results."

STEP 6: Clearly communicate your company's culture and values—and let employees participate in shaping them. The definition of company culture and values must be initiated by top management. Nevertheless, we know that the culture of an organization is by no means limited to what is defined at the higher levels. It is, in fact, what is lived and breathed in the daily environment, even in our current virtual working world.

By now, we are also cognizant that commitment and engagement are intimately connected with the level of participation in the process. Connecting the dots, it means that while top management may have the first and last word when it comes to culture and values, employees need to participate meaningfully in defining and publicizing these crucial aspects of the workplace.

Many of the processes we've suggested leaders should rely on to reduce bias can also be practiced by employees. Clear, organization-wide communication of the enormous value of bias eradication and the destructive role biases can play in employee and corporate performance, along with nudge-style suggestions for solutions, will incentivize workers at all levels to proactively combat their own and others' biases as a fundamental aspect of participating in company culture/values.

Are You Ready to Tackle Your Biases?

Most of the big corporate players, especially giant technology enterprises like Google, have been working on bias for years now. But, as many of these forward-thinking companies have learned, merely saying "we're against biases" doesn't work. It's important to know enough about our brains to work sensitively and effectively. In particular, we must find compelling, memorable ways to take that crucial step back, so that the less reactive parts of our brains get a chance to take command. A holistic awareness of our current rapidly evolving, tech-driven VUCA circumstances is also imperative, if we want to address bias in ways that will work in our fast-paced, evolving environments. As Fiona Macfarlane, chief inclusion officer at Ernst & Young, has explained, "In a complex, knowledge-driven economy, there are no longer solutions to problems, there are perspectives on dilemmas."

To reiterate, the more perspectives we have, the better. We know today that diverse teams comprising *and actively including* people from a variety of backgrounds are the most innovative—and the most successful. Thus, the motto of the European Union—"United in Diversity"—is one we would do well to integrate into our leadership. We all see the world differently—and that's fantastic! We must work together, listen to each other, respect our differences, and learn how to integrate and leverage those differences for optimal performance, not to mention healthier relationships. As we do so, we are literally rewiring our brains so that System 2 becomes ascendant, reinforcing the connection between differences and benefits.

These days, our differences literally translate into profit. They are the primary way to increase both our opportunities for success at work and our chances of making better decisions. All the while, our human variety boosts agility, creativity, knowledge, and so much more. We only need to get beyond our out-of-date biases to open our brains to these wonderful possibilities. To paraphrase Alvin Toffler, writer and noted futurist, the illiterate of the modern era will not be those who cannot read and write, but those who cannot learn, unlearn, and relearn.

Above all, leaders must be fluent in these crucial twenty-first-century skills. They must themselves constantly progress by unlearning old habits and ideas and replacing them with new, improved information and actions... and then use that knowledge to help their teams do the same. The tools you have learned in these final two chapters are designed to make this refreshing cycle possible. They enable the most evolved parts of our brains to be in command by consistently growing the power and influence of System 2. Counteracting—unlearning—biases allows us to forge better interpersonal connections and thereby spark more original ideas, fruitful collaborations, and innovative, adaptive solutions for true twenty-first-century professional literacy.

Neuroscience at Work

THANK YOU FOR joining me on a constructive and enlightening journey through the neuroscience of management. None of the small shifts and habits I've shared in this text requires a great deal of time or energy. Yet these microsteps can literally rewire your brains, at once avoiding or muting the neural circuitry that limits you and amplifying your neurological strengths.

Such practices are absolutely essential to exceptional leadership in our times. We've faced seismic changes during and after an unprecedented global pandemic. We continue to deal with the ongoing challenges of digital and societal transformations. In this VUCA environment, effective tools that enable us to evolve in our careers—and thereby support others' evolution—are priceless. Once you begin to diligently practice the exercises I've shared, you'll be well on your way to becoming the brain-smart leader twenty-first-century corporations need now and into the future.

I want to sum up the crucial takeaways from each chapter, to give your brains additional familiarity with the lessons we've learned. But I also want to be very clear that each and every brain technique is in some way interrelated. This means, for example, that the work we do on fostering a healthy delight in change translates into habits that will enable us to better mitigate bias in the workplace. It means that when we practice stepping away from context shifting and multitasking in an effort to shift from overwhelmed to thriving in our work lives, we also step toward creating a culture that fosters a healthier and more productive mindset. As a bonus, many of these techniques will help you evolve as a human being, too.

Here, in conclusion, are some key messages from every chapter. I've briefly summarized the central points of each—and reiterated why the information and practices covered matter. Together, these lessons reflect the vast potential and power of deploying neuroscience in leadership. You can dip into this section as a quick refresher for your Five Brain Leadership neuromanagement skills, or read (and re-read) it to sum up and reinforce the knowledge and skills you've built over the course of reading this book.

The Fundamentals of Five Brain Leadership

Chapter 1: Leverage All of Your Brains for Excellence at Work

When you get to know all of the components of your five (or five-plus!) brains, you'll know which parts are likely to be at the fore in any given situation. And you'll begin to grasp the wonderful complexity and myriad possibilities our fascinating brains embody. While we still have an enormous amount to learn, we have enough neuroscientific knowledge right now to contribute immeasurably to our managerial skill sets. The neuromanagement techniques throughout this book rely on extensive information about how our brains function to facilitate genuine progress.

Return to Chapter 1 to remind yourself of the strengths and challenges of our diverse brains. The brain basics explored in this chapter explain the unique roles each of your brains plays in your thoughts, actions, decision-making, and more. This introductory overview will help you make the best of each component, in part by nurturing vital connections between your various brains. And it will enable you to understand the reasoning behind the practices shared in subsequent chapters, all of which are designed to allow you to use neuroscience-based tools to simultaneously increase your self-awareness and boost your business acumen—for yourself, your team, and your organization.

Chapter 1 also reminds us that incorporating our feelings is crucial to achieving the ultimate in workplace excellence. After all, "emotion" and "motivation" have the same Latin root: *movere* or "to take action." I've intentionally designed the approaches in this book to honor the fact that four out of five of our brains are strongly linked with instincts and emotions, in order to reliably inspire positive actions and results.

Chapter 2: Honor Natural Physiological Cycles for Better Performance

Stressed out? Join the club. Unless, perhaps, you'd like to follow a happier, more robust path than the hectic, miserable status quo? Why, then you've come to the right place! Go to this chapter when you find yourself sinking back into habitual overload mode.

Here, we learned that it's possible to use the latest findings from neuroscience and human physiology, plus some time-tested wisdom, to shift our inner states from "quiet desperation" to truly flourishing. We debunked the myth of time management and replaced it with facts about how our brains actually work. We explored the science behind stress, and the difference between our natural stress response (the normal and essential stress reactions that enable us to deal with daily life) and the *distress* caused by the ceaseless busyness of contemporary work life. And we began to consider how finding ways to tune into our chronobiological rhythms can greatly improve our functioning at work and beyond.

Chapter 3: Use Bio-Hacks to Bring Your Work World Into Sync with Your Biology

The innovative yet practical ways to approach our daily scheduling covered in this chapter expand on the science introduced in Chapter 2 to give you a series of eight concrete, pragmatic tactics that will subtly, over time, disrupt your unhealthy physiological habits. These brain-healthy practices are designed to shift you from the red, chronically overwhelmed end of the stress curve to a state of flourishing, growing, green wellness. We achieve the latter by using science-based hacks to align all five of our brains with our biological cycles, thereby addressing anxiety, developing awareness, reducing unnecessary multitasking, implementing healthy rituals, and more—all with an eye toward optimizing our workplace productivity, efficiency, relationships, and, yes, contentment.

The tips in this chapter complement those in the following chapters, and will greatly enhance all of our combined neuromanagement efforts. As a bonus, implementing these habits can help us feel about a million percent happier as human beings.

Chapter 4: Educate Yourself on the Neuroscience of Change

We've been in a vortex of organizational, societal, and global transformation since the digital realm's early expansion. Some of our brains aren't too keen on the newfangled policies, ideas, processes, people, and so on that come with all that change. But constant change is here to stay. And leaders—and corporations—must evolve just to stay relevant, never mind get ahead. A deep understanding of why we react the way we do, with special attention on our fear circuitry, can help us foster sustainable approaches to change management.

Turn to the knowledge and tools in this chapter to soothe your five brains' nervous reactions and inspire yourself to train all of your brains to welcome transformation as a positive, creative, *necessary* aspect of workplace success. You truly can learn to circumvent your amygdala's primitive fear reactions and embrace—and profit from—the benefits of progress and innovation.

Chapter 5: Manage Change Constructively

When you know how to proactively deal with change, you can harness the power of choosing which changes to make and how to best handle them. While Chapter 4 featured lessons on how our brains react to change, Chapter 5 reveals brain-smart methods for tackling change at the organizational level.

Training our brains to overcome barriers to transformation by using targeted tactics to build and fortify neuroplasticity enables us to gladly and effectively think about, initiate, and execute changes for the good of the company, our teams, ourselves. We also learned that it's never too late to build neural resilience and agility, since we produce new neurons throughout our lives!

Use my Six Steps to Brain-Smart Corporate Change to reap the many tangible rewards of changing your and your employees' brains to grow your organization. You'll see that taking this measured, insightful, flexible approach will render your corporate change processes less chaotic and anxiety-provoking for your team, while also resulting in increased employee buy-in and improved results.

Chapter 6: Cultivate the Right Attitude for Progress

Our fundamental assumptions, beliefs, and attitudes—that is, our mindsets—shape our lives much more than we realize. As leaders, our beliefs, in particular those about talent and intelligence and effort, drive our own work habits along with our managerial style, our communications, and more. Surfacing those underlying mindsets and then replacing them with more productive, positive ones will have repercussions in every area covered in this book.

The neuroscience-based tweaks I've come up with will proactively take your self-awareness and attitude to the next level. Go to Chapter 6 when you want to remind yourself why and how we must strive mindfully to nurture a growth mindset (GM) by creating and reinforcing neural pathways that uplift and encourage us, and that enable us to see the possibility and potential in every situation.

Chapter 7: Lead with Your Most Productive Mindset

Of course, you're here to shine as a leader, so you'll want to know how to extend the personal and professional and corporate rewards of a growth mindset to your team.

At the group level, mindset is reflected in the atmosphere and expectations of the work environment, that is, in corporate culture. And it's discernable in people's communication styles, too. While a GM work environment may seem elusive, there are tangible and effective ways to support genuine positive advances in the attitudes and, therefore, actions and interactions, of those under your leadership.

Turn to Chapter 7 for tools to bring the best out in your team over the long term. You'll start by simply paying attention, together. Over time and with practice, a more positive, fruitful GM orientation—in the form of a learning culture—will begin to prevail in your workplace. In turn, your team of active, confident, mutually supportive learners will bring perseverance, agility, and meaningful growth to the business.

Chapter 8: Know Your Biases

All of the brain-expanding we've done so far has, I hope, prepared you for some of the most important work you'll ever do. Of course, like many others, managers typically think they are above bias. In this chapter, we learned how damagingly untrue that belief is, via an exploration of the ubiquity and unconscious neurological roots of these totally insidious "mindbugs."

As is the case with many of our ingrained, unconscious neurological responses, biases evolved as a tool for self-preservation. They're at the ready to vigilantly and rapidly protect us in our decision-making, interactions, communications… well, pretty much every time we encounter another person, form an opinion, or make a choice!

When you need to review the brain science behind bias, and revisit ways to activate the parts of our brains that can mitigate its effects, you'll find everything you need in this chapter. Dive in when you want to downgrade System 1 and get System 2 on the front burner. You'll find abundant justification for challenging your own perceptions and subconscious assumptions, as well as practices that build on and connect to earlier brain-smart efforts. You'll also find insights to help you begin "cleaning" the lens through which you see the world, thereby becoming a more agile, fair, innovative, productive, inclusive leader. Think that sounds too optimistic? Re-read the chapter!

Chapter 9: Mitigate Bias to Nurture Genuine, Dynamic Workplace Connections

We cannot eliminate biases, but we can counteract them so effectively that we in essence take an evolutionary leap past our automatic responses to something much, much better. And it all starts with the willingness to pause and take a step back for a little metacognition (thinking about our thinking).

As leaders, team/company culture and values are of the utmost importance to us, and a central aspect of what we work on. Our differences should be celebrated and leaders are the ones who can, and *must*, make that attitude the workplace norm. Only by actively addressing and transcending biases can we truly develop diversity and inclusion, innovation and flexibility, in short, the necessary skills to thrive in the twenty-first century.

How? Flip back to Chapter 9 for personal-, team-, and organizational-level toolkits for bias mitigation. The resulting improvements in connections won't just manifest on the human plane—they will bring enormous benefits to the business as well.

Five Brain Leadership in Practice

Over the course of reading these nine chapters and trying out their various exercises, you've gained significant amateur neuro-expertise at a scale and depth that would have been unthinkable just decades ago. You've grown as a leader—and as a human being.

The information you've taken to heart and the abilities you've conscientiously honed are absolutely essential to business success in our VUCA era. When we call upon the less reactive, more evolved parts of our brains, we empower ourselves to learn, and—crucially—unlearn, in ways that drive fluency and agility in neuromanagement. The results? Well, there are too many to count. Abundant organizational productivity, stronger, healthier teams, and improved self-awareness are just a few of the outcomes of skilled neuromanagement based on a high level of knowledge of all five of our incredible brains.

So, where do you go from here? My goal is that, after reading this book, you will change the components of your lens. Remember that we see the world as *we* are—and so we can change our understanding of how we see the world. Now that you have more information about how our different brains work and how they affect our behavior, you are in the position to gain a deeper understanding of the causes of our decisions—both those of others and of your own—as well as how to relate to others and how to talk with your people to generate greater commitment. I would be delighted to continue to accompany you on this journey. Count on me!

CARLOS

Acknowledgments

WHERE TO START...

Getting to this point of publishing a book implies that there has been a path. Defining the milestones that allowed me to achieve this great goal is not easy. I can identify several, but there is not enough room in any book to name them all.

From the professional side, starting from when I came to live to Europe, there are many people to be grateful for, starting from Manuel Tallada with his inexhaustible and successful MRC project, where I found the possibility to discover and reinvent myself professionally in my new home, up to Ron Dahms, former owner and CEO of Optimum Talent, who opened the door to a quantum leap experience in my professional and personal life. He had the vision and the courage to make it a reality by inviting me to bring my work on neuro-management to Canada, where I spent seven amazing years of my life. I have a very special mention for Dr. Larry Cash, whom I consider to be a genius for his professional work. He not only believed in me and gave me his friendship, he also gave me the honor of becoming the co-author of his master-piece, *Personality DNA: Discover Your True Personality.*

I also would like to refer to a professional experience that I have been developing for more than a decade now, which is teaching neuromanagement in the MBA program at the University of New York in Prague (UNYP). Every year I learn more, and giving these classes to powerful young profession-als who challenge me at every moment is a permanent source of energy and joy. I really love it! Thank you to Sotiris Karagi-annis, director of the program and a great friend.

Coming to this book itself, I'll start by thanking Jennifer Elizabeth Brunton, a top professional editor in the scientific, business, and academic worlds. Jennifer started out as my editor, but along the way we discovered that we shared many of the ideas, concepts, and values expressed in the book—so much so that she became more of a collaborator. Her material has enriched my original book immensely. Thanks, Jenny, so much!

I also want to thank Phil Buckley, an expert in change, music, and friendship. He was my last push to move for-ward with this book through Page Two. This company has become the best partner ever to publish a book, thanks to Trena, Adrineh, Melissa, Chris, Peter, and those who worked behind the scenes and with whom I never even had direct contact. What an amazing team of professionals! They made me feel completely under care and confident that I was per-fectly guided in the complicated and exhausting path of launching a book.

And, last but not least, I want to acknowledge the key emotional support that helped me reach this moment in my life—starting with my biggest fan ever, my father, with all his unconditional love and permanent support. Thanks, Dad: I want these words to reach you in whatever reality you find yourself in now. And moving to my current family, thanks to all of my children, who, through their own individual richness, taught me and still are teaching me so much. And especially to my wife, Irina, an outstanding person, an amazing professional, and an incomparable and essential life road companion.

Notes

Introduction

p. 5   *"seeks to harness science across multiple disciplines...* James Olds, "For an International Decade of the Mind," *Malaysian Journal of Medical Sciences* 18(2), April/June 2011, pubmed.ncbi.nlm.nih .gov/22135580; and Manfred Spitzer, "Decade of the Mind," *Philosophy, Ethics, and Humanities in Medicine* 3(7), February 20, 2008, doi.org/10.1186/1747-5341-3-7.

Chapter 1: How Many Brains Does It Take to Run an Organization?

p. 12   *for his work on the split brain...* NobelPrize.org, "Roger W. Sperry—Facts," nobelprize.org/prizes/medicine/1981/sperry.

p. 12   *a map of language in the brain...* Alexander G. Huth, Wendy A. de Heer, Thomas L. Griffiths, Frédéric E. Theunissen, and Jack L. Gallant, "Natural Speech Reveals the Semantic Maps That Tile Human Cerebral Cortex," *Nature* 532(7600), April 27, 2016, doi.org/10.1038/nature17637.

p. 13   *process of evolution did not replace earlier brains...* Paul MacLean, *The Triune Brain in Evolution: Role in Paleocerebral Functions* (Plenum Press, 1990).

p. 16   *presence of thousands of neurons in the heart...* J. Andrew Armour, "Intrinsic Cardiac Neurons," *Journal of Cardiovascular Electrophysiology* 2(4), August 1991, doi.org/10.1111/ j.1540-8167.1991.tb01330.x.

p. 17   *experience major depression...* Simha Ravven, Caroline
         Bader, Armin Azar, and James Rudolph, "Depressive Symptoms
         After CABG Surgery: A Meta-Analysis," *Harvard Review
         of Psychiatry* 21(2), March/April 2013, doi.org/10.1097/
         HRP.0b013e31828a3612.

p. 17   *describes how the Dalai Lama introduced him...* Richard
         Davidson with Sharon Begley, *The Emotional Life of Your Brain:
         How Its Unique Patterns Affect the Way You Think, Feel, and Live—
         and How You Can Change Them* (Hudson Street Press, 2012).

p. 19   *"The [gut] brain doesn't help with the great thought processes...*
         Michael Gershon, *The Second Brain: A Groundbreaking New
         Understanding of Nervous Disorders of the Stomach and Intestine*
         (Harper Perennial, 1999).

p. 19   *"Thus equipped with its own reflexes and senses...* Adam Hadhazy,
         "Think Twice: How the Gut's 'Second Brain' Influences
         Mood and Well-Being," *Scientific American*, February 12, 2010,
         scientificamerican.com/article/gut-second-brain.

p. 19   *90 percent of our serotonin...* Australian Spinal Research
         Foundation, "Listen to Your Gut Part 1: The Second
         Brain," August 9, 2016, spinalresearch.com.au/
         listen-gut-part-1-second-brain.

p. 20   *our rational and emotional brains have to be connected...*
         Antonio Damasio, *Descartes' Error: Emotion, Reason, and the
         Human Brain* (Penguin, 2005).

p. 22   *We humans tend to think of emotions...* Temple Grandin and
         Catherine Johnson, *Animals in Translation: Using the Mysteries of
         Autism to Decode Animal Behavior* (Simon & Schuster, 2005).

p. 22   *"The essential difference between emotion and reason...* Science.ca,
         "Medicine—Donald Brian Calne," September 17, 2015,
         science.ca/scientists/scientistprofile.php?pID=327.

p. 23   *Business decisions are rarely black and white...* Grant Thornton,
         "About Us," grantthornton.tw/en/about/an-instinct-for-growth.

p. 23   *"What is technology for...* Grupo Motor Gómez, "Nuevo Spot
         Audi A4 Advanced Edition," YouTube video, posted June 15,
         2013, youtube.com/watch?v=Zmag2QaQCPk.

Chapter 2: From Overwhelmed to Flourishing

p. 31   *describes a* Health Psychology *study...* Kelly McGonigal,
         *The Upside of Stress: Why Stress Is Good for You, and How
         to Get Good at It* (Penguin Random House, 2016).

p. 39   *Selye's work delved into the adaptive capacities…*
Paul Rosch, "Reminiscences of Hans Selye, and the
Birth of 'Stress,'" American Institute of Stress, stress.org/
about/hans-selye-birth-of-stress.

p. 43   *normally, our brain demands 20 percent…* Ferris Jabr, "Does
Thinking Really Hard Burn More Calories?" *Scientific American*,
July 18, 2012, scientificamerican.com/article/thinking-hard-
calories; and Marcus Raichle and Debra Gusnard, "Appraising
the Brain's Energy Budget," *Proceedings of the National
Academy of Sciences* 99(16), August 6, 2002, doi.org/10.1073/
pnas.172399499.

p. 43   *"A great deal of meaningful activity…* Marcus Raichle, Ann Mary
MacLeod, Abraham Snyder, William Powers, Debra Gusnard,
and Gordon Shulman, "A Default Mode of Brain Function,"
Proceedings of the National Academy of Sciences 98(2), January
2001, doi.org/10.1073/pnas.98.2.676.

p. 45   *the main features of these two key networks…* George Siegel,
Bernard Agranoff, Wayne Albers, Stephen Fisher, and Michael
Uhler, eds., *Basic Neurochemistry, 6th Edition: Molecular, Cellular
and Medical Aspects* (Lippincott-Raven, 1999); ncbi.nlm
.nih.gov/books/NBK20385; and Jonathan Power, Alexander
Cohen, Steven Nelson, Gagan Wig, Kelly Anne Barnes,
Jessica Church, Alecia Vogel, Timothy Laumann, Fran Miezin,
Bradley Schlaggar, and Steven Petersen, "Functional Network
Organization of the Human Brain," *Neuron* 72(4), November 17,
2011, doi.org/10.1016/j.neuron.2011.09.006.

p. 49   *the impact of taking twenty-minute post-lunch breaks…* David
F. Dinges, Martin T. Orne, Wayne G. Whitehouse, and
Emily C. Orne, "Temporal Placement of a Nap for Alertness:
Contributions of Circadian Phase and Prior Wakefulness,"
Sleep 10(4), July 1987, doi.org/10.1093/SLEEP/10.4.313.

p. 49   *feel more pressure to not take a lunch break…* Tork USA,
"Take Back the Lunch Break," torkusa.com/torkcampaigns/
take-back-the-lunch-break.

p. 50   *connecting naps with improved working memory in astronauts…*
NASA Science, "NASA Naps," June 3, 2005, science.nasa.gov/
science-news/science-at-nasa/2005/03jun_naps.

p. 50   *now support nap-taking in the workplace…* Dan Ketchum,
"You Can Nap on the Job at These 10 Companies,"
GoBankingRates.com, February 5, 2019, gobankingrates.com/
money/jobs/companies-allow-napping-at-work.

p. 51   *the 2017 Nobel Prize in Physiology or Medicine was awarded...*
Bill Chappell, "Nobel Prize in Medicine Is Awarded
to 3 Americans for Work on Circadian Rhythm," *The
Two-Way* (blog), National Public Radio, October 2, 2017,
npr.org/sections/thetwo-way/2017/10/02/554993385/
nobel-prize-in-medicine-is-awarded-to-3-americans-for-
work-on-circadian-rhythm.

Chapter 3: Flourishing at Work

p. 56   *anxiety can only manifest when...* Lisa Firestone, "5 Truths
about Anxiety to Help You Stay Present," *Psychology Today*,
July 3, 2018, psychologytoday.com/us/blog/compassion-
matters/201807/5-truths-about-anxiety-help-you-stay-present.

p. 57   *the "5-4-3-2-1 coping technique...* Sara Smith, "5-4-3-2-1
Coping Technique for Anxiety," *Behavioral Health Partners Blog*,
University of Rochester Medical Center, April 10, 2018,
urmc.rochester.edu/behavioral-health-partners/bhp-blog/
april-2018/5-4-3-2-1-coping-technique-for-anxiety.aspx.

p. 65   *known as the ABC model...* Albert Ellis and Robert Harper,
A Guide to Rational Living (Prentice-Hall, 1961).

p. 66   *"Be careful how you are talking to yourself...* Lisa Hayes,
lisamhayes.com.

p. 70   *It reduces smaller gray-matter density...* Kep Kee Loh and Ryota
Kanai, "Higher Media Multi-tasking Activity Is Associated with
Smaller Gray-Matter Density in the Anterior Cingulate Cortex,"
PLoS One 9(9), September 24, 2014, doi.org/10.1371/journal
.pone.0106698.

p. 70   *It leads to increased anxiety...* Olivia Goldhill, "Neuroscientists
Say Multitasking Literally Drains the Energy Reserves
of Your Brain," *Quartz*, July 3, 2016, qz.com/722661/
neuroscientists-say-multitasking-literally-drains-the-energy-
reserves-of-your-brain.

p. 70   *It impacts your short-term memory...* Wesley C. Clapp, Michael
T. Rubens, Jasdeep Sabharwal, and Adam Gazzaley, "Deficit in
Switching between Functional Brain Networks Underlies the
Impact of Multitasking on Working Memory in Older Adults,"
Proceedings of the National Academy of Sciences 108(17), March 8,
2011, doi.org/10.1073/pnas.1015297108.

p. 70　*It inhibits creative thinking...* Eyal Ophir, Clifford Nass, and Anthony Wagner, "Cognitive Control in Media Multitaskers," *Psychological and Cognitive Sciences* 106(37), September 15, 2009, doi.org/10.1073/pnas.0903620106.

p. 71　*It stops you from getting into a state of flow...* Corinna Peifer and Gina Zipp, "All at Once? The Effects of Multitasking Behavior on Flow and Subjective Performance," *European Journal of Work and Organizational Psychology* 28(5), July 13, 2019, doi.org/10.1080/1359432X.2019.1647168.

p. 71　*It causes more mistakes and less productivity...* Travis Bradberry, "Multitasking Damages Your Brain and Your Career, New Studies Suggest," TalentSmartEQ, talentsmarteq.com/articles/Multitasking-Damages-Your-Brain-and-Your-Career,-New-Studies-Suggest-2102500909-p-1.html; Gisela Telis, "Multitasking Splits the Brain," *Science*, April 15, 2010, science.org/content/article/multitasking-splits-brain-rev2; and John Hamilton, "Think You're Multitasking? Think Again," *Morning Edition*, National Public Radio, October 2, 2008, npr.org/2008/10/02/95256794/think-youre-multitasking-think-again.

p. 74　*the need for rituals is a basic human instinct...* Francesca Gino and Michael Norton, "Why Rituals Work," *Scientific American*, May 14, 2013, scientificamerican.com/article/why-rituals-work.

p. 74　*"We agree that life is full of uncertainty...* Nick Hobson, "The Anxiety-Busting Properties of Ritual," *Psychology Today*, September 25, 2017, psychologytoday.com/us/blog/ritual-and-the-brain/201709/the-anxiety-busting-properties-ritual.

p. 76　*created a program called PERMA...* Martin Seligman, *Flourish: A Visionary New Understanding of Happiness and Well-Being* (Atria Books, 2012).

Chapter 4: Train Your Brain to Tackle Organizational Transformation with Gusto

p. 86　*"Everything flows...* Patrick Hanks, William T. McLeod, and Laurence Urdang, eds. *Collins English Dictionary* (Collins, 1979).

p. 90　*brain represents about 2 percent of our total body mass...* Nikhil Swaminathan, "Why Does the Brain Need So Much Power?" *Scientific American*, April 29, 2008, scientificamerican.com/article/why-does-the-brain-need-s.

p. 98   *"stages of grief" described by Elisabeth Kübler-Ross*... Jodi Clarke, "The Five Stages of Grief," VeryWell Mind, updated February 12, 2021, verywellmind.com/five-stages-of-grief-4175361.

Chapter 5: Brain-Smart Organizational Change

p. 108   *the term "neuroplasticity" was first used in 1948*... Jerzy Konorski, *Conditioned Reflexes and Neuron Organization*, translated by Stephen Garry (Cambridge University Press, 1948).

p. 108   *be the sculptor of his own brain*... Rodolfo Llinás, "The Contribution of Santiago Ramón y Cajal to Functional Neuroscience," *Nature Reviews Neuroscience* 4(1), January 2003, doi.org/10.1038/nrn1011.

p. 109   *"Everything can be taken from a man but one thing*... Viktor Frankl, *Man's Search for Meaning* (Beacon Press, 1959).

p. 110   *three main types of "food" that allow neurons to make connections*... Belal Shohayeb, Mohamed Diab, Mazen Ahmed, and Dominic Chi Hiung Ng, "Factors That Influence Adult Neurogenesis as Potential Therapy," *Translational Neurodegeneration* 7(4), February 21, 2018, doi.org/10.1186/s40035-018-0109-9.

p. 111   *negative attitudes basically kill baby neurons*... Natalie Marchant, Lise Lovland, Rebecca Jones, Alexa Pichet Binette, Julie Gonneaud, Eider Arenaza-Urquijo, Gael Chételat, and Sylvia Villeneuve, "Repetitive Negative Thinking Is Associated with Amyloid, Tau, and Cognitive Decline," *Alzheimer's & Dementia* 16(7), July 2020, doi.org/10.1002/alz.12116; and Kristen Lindquist, Ajay Satpute, Tor Wager, Jochen Weber, and Lisa Feldman Barrett, "The Brain Basis of Positive and Negative Affect: Evidence from a Meta-analysis of the Human Neuroimaging Literature," *Cerebral Cortex* 26(5), January 28, 2015, doi.org/10.1093/cercor/bhv001.

p. 112   *they are highly contagious*... Stephen Dimmock and William Gerken, "Research: How One Bad Employee Can Corrupt a Whole Team," *Harvard Business Review*, March 5, 2018, hbr.org/2018/03/research-how-one-bad-employee-can-corrupt-a-whole-team.

p. 113   *we can be positive most or all of the time*... Jennifer Post, "How to Develop a Positive Attitude in the Workplace," *Business News Daily*, updated December 10, 2021, businessnewsdaily.com/6912-develop-positive-mindset.html; and Courtney E. Ackerman, "What Is Positive Mindset: 89 Ways to Achieve a Positive Mental Attitude," *Positive Psychology*, updated March 28, 2022, positivepsychology.com/positive-mindset.

p. 119   *creates an emotional connection with the product...* Michael Norton, Daniel Mochon, and Dan Ariely, "The IKEA Effect: When Labor Leads to Love," *Journal of Consumer Psychology* 22(3), July 2012, doi.org/10.1016/j.jcps.2011.08.002.

p. 121   *ongoing, small, incremental steps toward the goal...* Jeff Kavanaugh and Rafee Tarafdar, "Break Down Change Management into Small Steps," *Harvard Business Review*, May 3, 2021, hbr.org/2021/05/break-down-change-management-into-small-steps.

p. 123   *Schwartz developed the following formula...* David Rock and Jeffrey Schwartz, "The Neuroscience of Leadership," *strategy+business* 43, May 30, 2006, strategy-business.com/article/06207.

p. 124   *A strong, inspiring vision can be an immensely powerful tool...* The Business Practitioner, "The Power of a Compelling Vision," April 14, 2015, thebusinesspractitioner.com/the-power-of-a-compelling-vision; and Jeffrey Gandz, "Compelling Visions: Content, Context, Credibility, and Collaboration," *Ivey Business Journal*, March/April 2009, iveybusinessjournal.com/publication/compelling-visions-content-context-credibility-and-collaboration.

Chapter 6: Impactful Mindset

p. 136   *A few modern philosophers assert that an individual's intelligence...* Alfred Binet and Théodore Simon, *The Development of Intelligence in Children: The Binet-Simon Scale*, translated by Elizabeth S. Kite (Williams & Wilkins, 1973; 1916).

p. 138   *Take the fascinating example of Elon Musk...* Ashlee Vance, *Elon Musk: Tesla, SpaceX, and the Quest for a Fantastic Future* (HarperCollins, 2015).

p. 138   *Richard Branson, who is dyslexic...* Richard Branson, *Screw It, Let's Do It: Lessons in Life and Business* (Virgin Books, 2007).

p. 138   *J.K. Rowling's first manuscript was rejected twelve times...* Anjelica Oswald, "J.K. Rowling Shares Photos of Her Rejection Letters for 'Inspiration,'" *Business Insider*, March 25, 2016, businessinsider.com/jk-rowling-rejection-letters-2016-3.

p. 140   *identify the composition of the complete human genome...*
Heidi Chial, "DNA Sequencing Technologies Key to the
Human Genome Project," *Nature Education* 1(1), 2008,
nature.com/scitable/topicpage/dna-sequencing-technologies-
key-to-the-human-828.

p. 140   *Conrad Waddington coined the term "epigenetics"...* Aaron
Goldberg, C. David Allis, and Emily Bernstein, "Epigenetics:
A Landscape Takes Shape," *Cell* 128(4), February 23, 2007,
doi.org/10.1016/j.cell.2007.02.006.

p. 143   *differences in the way children tended to face new challenges...*
Carol Dweck, *Mindset: The New Psychology of Success* (Random
House, 2006).

Chapter 7: Leading with Your Most Productive Mindset

p. 155   *Stephen Karpman's "drama triangle" model...* Stephen Karpman,
karpmandramatriangle.com.

p. 157   *employees operating from an FM narrative...* Chris Miller,
"Expectations Create Outcomes: Growth Mindsets in
Organizations," UNC Kenan-Flagler Business School
Executive Development, 2016, available at homepages.se.edu/
cvonbergen/files/2019/05/expectations-create-outcomes.pdf.

p. 163   *leadership is very keen to cultivate a learning culture...*
Karla Gutierrez, "The Google Way of Building a Strong
Learning Culture," SHIFT e-Learning, shiftelearning.com/
blog/building-learning-culture.

p. 163   *"the learning curve is...* Josh Bersin, "The Use of MOOCs and
Online Education Is Exploding: Here's Why," JoshBersin.com,
December 30, 2015, joshbersin.com/2015/12/the-use-of-
moocs-and-online-education-is-exploding-heres-why.

p. 163   *"Learning cultures improve employee engagement...* Tala Nabong,
"Creating a Learning Culture for the Improvement of Your
Organization," Training Industry, April 7, 2015, trainingindustry
.com/articles/workforce-development/creating-a-learning-
culture-for-the-improvement-of-your-organization.

p. 163   *some common misconceptions or myths...* Heidi Grant, Mary
Slaughter, and Andrea Derler, "5 Mistakes Companies Make
about Growth Mindsets," *Harvard Business Review*, July 23,
2018, hbr.org/2018/07/5-mistakes-companies-make-about-
growth-mindsets.

p. 164   *GM employees are more likely to...* HBR Editors, "How
Companies Can Profit from a 'Growth Mindset,'"
Harvard Business Review, November 2014, hbr.org/2014/11/
how-companies-can-profit-from-a-growth-mindset.

Chapter 8: Are You a Biased Leader?

p. 180   *This tool is condensed and adapted...* David McRaney,
You Are Not So Smart (Penguin Random House, 2012).

p. 188   *Kahneman has found that our brain reacts and responds...*
Daniel Kahneman, *Thinking, Fast and Slow* (Farrar, Straus
& Giroux, 2013).

p. 194   *"ingrained habits of thought that lead to errors...* Mahzarin R.
Banaji and Anthony G. Greenwald, *Blindspot: Hidden Biases of
Good People* (Delacorte Press, 2013).

p. 200   *a codex of more than two hundred biases...* Buster Benson,
"Cognitive Bias Cheat Sheet," *Better Humans*, September 1, 2016,
betterhumans.pub/cognitive-bias-cheat-sheet-55a472476b18.

p. 201   *Confirmation bias can impel us to make inferior decisions...*
Britannica, "Confirmation bias," britannica.com/science/
confirmation-bias.

p. 202   *our memories are not fixed...* Neal Roese and Kathleen Vohs,
"Hindsight Bias," *Perspectives on Psychological Science* 7(5),
September 5, 2012, doi.org/10.1177/1745691612454303.

p. 203   *the arguments that carry the greatest weight...* Behavioral
Economics, "Availability Heuristic," behavioraleconomics.com/
resources/mini-encyclopedia-of-be/availability-heuristic.

p. 203   *overestimate how much other people agree with us...* Lee Ross,
David Greene, and Pamela House, "The 'False Consensus
Effect': An Egocentric Bias in Social Perception and Attribution
Processes," *Journal of Experimental Social Psychology* 13(3),
May 1977, doi.org/10.1016/0022-1031(77)90049-X.

p. 204   *being seen as attractive and/or capable...* Al Ries, "Understanding
Marketing Psychology and the Halo Effect," *Ad Age*, April 17,
2006, adage.com/article/al-ries/understanding-marketing-
psychology-halo-effect/108676.

p. 204   *every inch an employee is above average height...* Timothy Judge
and Daniel Cable, "The Effect of Physical Height on Workplace
Success and Income: Preliminary Test of a Theoretical Model,"
Journal of Applied Psychology 89(3), June 2004,
doi.org/10.1037/0021-9010.89.3.428.

p. 204   *gender biases in two hundred performance review processes...*
Paola Cecchi-Dimeglio, "How Gender Bias Corrupts
Performance Reviews, and What to Do about It," *Harvard
Business Review*, April 12, 2017, hbr.org/2017/04/how-gender-
bias-corrupts-performance-reviews-and-what-to-do-about-it.

p. 205   *positive in a man and aggressive in a woman...* Pratima
Rao Gluckman, "When Women Are Called 'Aggressive'
at Work," *Forbes*, August 28, 2018, forbes.com/sites/
nextavenue/2018/08/28/when-women-are-called-aggressive-
at-work/?sh=65d26b97bc89.

Chapter 9: Mitigating Biases for Better Decisions, Relationships, and Results

p. 209   *subconsciously shapes our reactions to a new person...* Charles
Stangor, Rajiv Jhangiani, and Hammond Tarry, *Principles
of Social Psychology*, 1st International H5P Edition (BCcampus,
2011), available for free at opentextbc.ca/socialpsychology/
chapter/initial-impression-formation.

p. 209   *seeks out interests, skills, and background elements that match...*
Pennsylvania State University, "Similar-to-Me Effect in the
Workplace," *Psych 424 Blog*, April 17, 2015, sites.psu.edu/
aspsy/2015/04/17/similar-to-me-effect-in-the-workplace.

p. 211   *we tend to deem men more qualified than women...* International
Labour Organization, "Breaking Barriers: Unconscious Gender
Bias in the Workplace," ACT/EMP Research Note, August 2017,
ilo.org/wcmsp5/groups/public/---ed_dialogue/---act_emp/
documents/publication/wcms_601276.pdf.

p. 211   *orchestras began installing screens during auditions...* Claudia
Goldin and Cecilia Rouse, "Orchestrating Impartiality:
The Impact of 'Blind' Auditions on Female Musicians,"
American Economic Review 90(4), September 2000, jstor.org/
stable/117305.

p. 213   *"The vast majority of human decisions...* Daniel Kahneman,
Thinking, Fast and Slow (Farrar, Straus & Giroux, 2013).

p. 214   *Accessibility is being able...* Liz Fosslien and Mollie West Duffy,
*No Hard Feelings: The Secret Power of Embracing Emotions at
Work* (Portfolio, 2019).

p. 217   *may for others represent a deep offense...* Harriet W. Sheridan
Center for Teaching and Learning, Brown University,
"Micro-aggressions and Micro-Affirmations," Brown University,
brown.edu/sheridan/microaggressions-and-micro-
affirmations-0.

p. 218   *"tiny acts of opening doors to opportunity...* Mary Rowe, "Micro-
Affirmations and Micro-Inequities," *Journal of the International
Ombudsman Association* 1(1), 2008, available at studylib.net/
doc/8234804/micro-affirmations-and-micro-inequities.

p. 219   *"You can't be a great manager without...* Joan Williams and Sky
Mihaylo, "How the Best Bosses Interrupt Bias on Their Teams,"
Harvard Business Review, November–December 2019, hbr.org/
2019/11/how-the-best-bosses-interrupt-bias-on-their-teams.

p. 224   *"single statistical factor for a group that predicts...* 2U, "What Is
Collective Intelligence and Why Should You Use It?"
GetSmarter (blog), August 27, 2020, getsmarter.com/blog/
career-advice/what-is-collective-intelligence-and-why-should-
you-use-it.

p. 230   *one app that specializes in delivering these "nudges"...* Humu,
"How Nudges Work," humu.com/how-nudges-work.

p. 230   *in general, nudges help people...* Oksana Mont, Matthias
Lehner, and Eva Heiskanen, "Nudging: A Tool for
Sustainable Behaviour?" Swedish EPA Report 6643, 2014,
researchgate.net/publication/271211332_Nudging_
A_tool_for_sustainable_behaviour.

p. 233   *especially giant technology enterprises like Google...* re:Work
with Google, "Guide: Raise Awareness about Unconscious Bias,"
rework.withgoogle.com/guides/unbiasing-raise-awareness/
steps/watch-unconscious-bias-at-work.

p. 233   *"In a complex, knowledge-driven economy...* Erin Anderssen,
"How 'Unconscious Bias' Could Stand in the Way
of Your Promotion," *Globe and Mail*, October 30, 2014,
theglobeandmail.com/life/relationships/diversity-corporations-
studying-effects-of-unconscious-bias/article21384704.

Index

About the Authors

CARLOS DAVIDOVICH, MD, is a performance and executive coach with over twenty years of experience supporting the development of leaders and management teams alike on an international scale. Originally educated as a medical doctor and drawing on his management experience in business executive roles for multinational pharmaceutical companies such as F. Hoffmann-La Roche and Pharmacia/Pfizer, Davidovich combines his understanding of the brain and of business to deliver lectures, workshops, and coaching modalities that help his clients apply the principles of neuromanagement within their organizations to create sustainable change. As co-author of *Personality DNA: Discover Your True Personality*, he is also helping individuals succeed by gaining knowledge about their own unique character traits. Davidovich teaches in several MBA programs in Canada and Europe, and is a thought leader with the Institute of Coaching at McLean Hospital, a Harvard Medical School affiliate. He was raised and educated in Argentina and lived and worked for many years in Europe and in Canada before returning to Madrid, where he lives.

JENNIFER ELIZABETH BRUNTON, PHD, spent many years as a professor of ethics, bioethics, religion, and philosophy while working as a freelance editor on Fulbright proposals and academic books. Now a full-time writer/editor, she has worked with some of the most distinguished names in publishing, including *Forbes*, Random House, Content Innovo, and Mirabella. Brunton's recent book is *The #ActuallyAutistic Guide to Advocacy: Step-by-Step Advice on How to Ally and Speak Up with Autistic People and the Autism Community* (with Jenna Gensic).

Go Deeper into
Five Brain Leadership

HELLO TO ALL OF YOU WHO HAVE
JUST FINISHED READING THIS BOOK.

Having read this far, I can assume that you found the material interesting. I would like to offer you more ways to keep our relationship growing, and to help spread the fascinating area of knowledge that is neuromanagement.

HERE ARE A FEW THINGS YOU CAN DO:

1 **GROUP PURCHASES:** Contact me to find out about discounts and special offers that can help you buy copies of *Five Brain Leadership* for your entire team or organization. We can even partner to create a customized edition that includes a foreword from your CEO or other leader.

2 **INVITE ME TO YOUR EVENT:** I have a range of workshops, keynotes, and lectures on neuromanagement for organizations—including the ideas you discovered in this book and many more topics!

3 **WORKSHOPS:** A lecture can be inspirational but a workshop or a series of workshops is transformative. Let's work with the situations that are real for your own people. I will show you how to apply the knowledge to make positive change happen, and to make sure it lasts.

4　**EXECUTIVE AND PERFORMANCE COACHING SESSIONS:** My individual and team coaching processes apply the neuromanagement concepts you learned in this book. It's a completely different way to understand your unique working processes and to create effective and sustainable changes.

5　**EMAIL LIST:** Sign up on my website to receive the latest news in neuroscience applied to organizations and businesses. You'll also get access to my YouTube channel.

Finally, if you feel inspired enough to write a review, please do so on your favorite social media platform, reading community, or online retailer.

Here is how you can find me:
carlosdavidovich.com
brain@carlosdavidovich.com
linkedin.com/in/carlosdavidovich

CPSIA information can be obtained
at www.ICGtesting.com
Printed in the USA
BVHW071021230123
656884BV00018B/224

9 781774 582732